AF290972

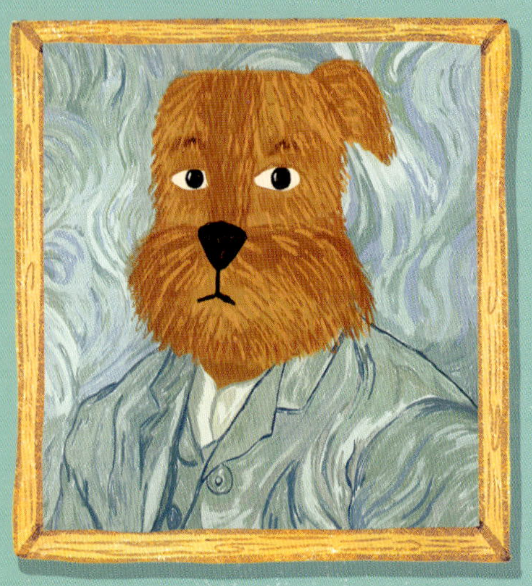

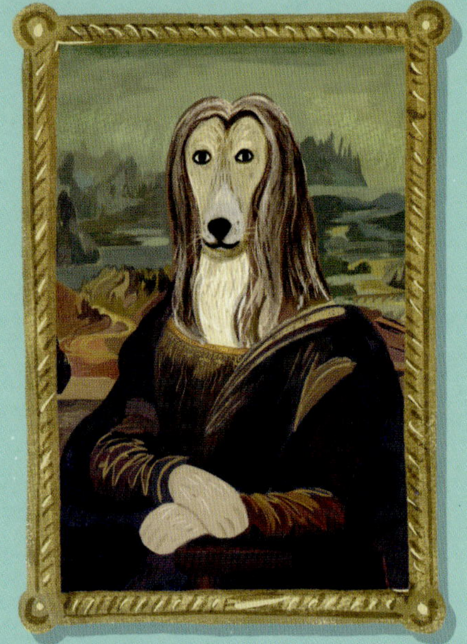

ILLUSTRATED BY
NIA GOULD

WRITTEN AND EDITED
BY JOCELYN NORBURY

DESIGNED BY BARBARA WARD
COVER DESIGN BY JOHN BIGWOOD

First published in Great Britain in 2025 by LOM ART, an imprint of
Michael O'Mara Books Limited, 9 Lion Yard, Tremadoc Road, London SW4 7NQ

W www.mombooks.com/lom
f Michael O'Mara Books
X @OMaraBooks
O @lomartbooks

A CIP catalogue record for this book is available from the British Library.

ISBN: 978-1-915751-27-0

2 4 6 8 10 9 7 5 3 1

Printed in March 2025 by Leo Paper Products Ltd, Heshan Astros
Printing Limited, Xuantan Temple Industrial Zone, Gulao
Town, Heshan City, Guangdong Province, China.

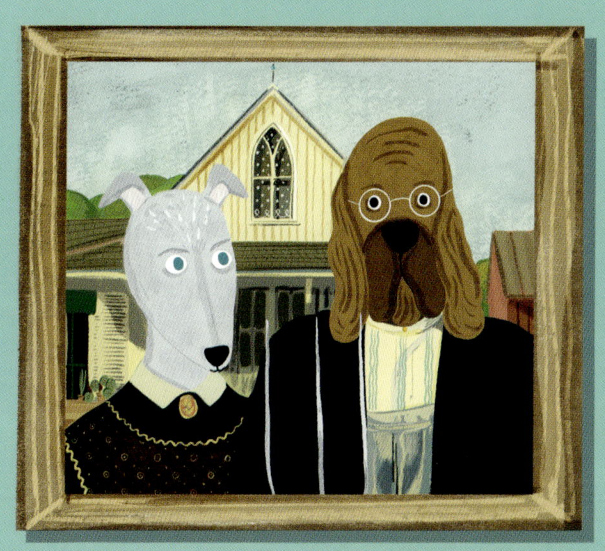

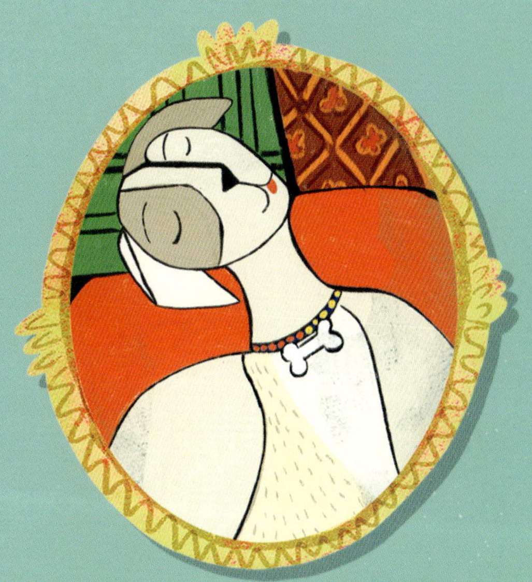

A HISTORY OF PORTRAITS
IN 21 DOGS

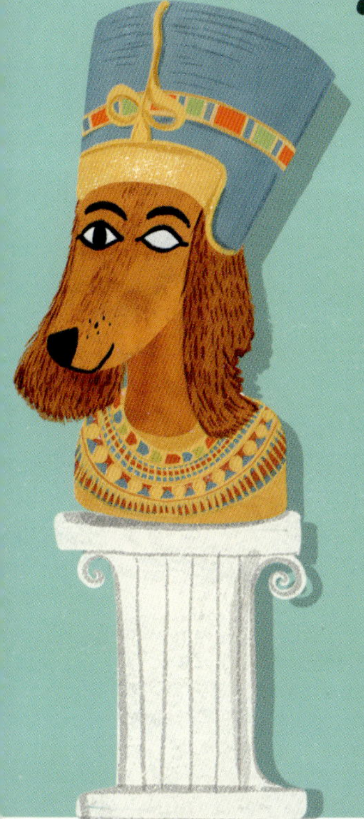

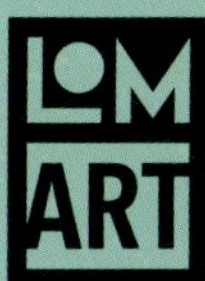

INTRODUCTION

Portraiture is an art form as old as art itself – artists have been capturing human likenesses for millennia. From busts to bronzes, oil paintings to photographs, portraits have long been used as status symbols, as a means for self-expression and as a reflection of the world that we live in.

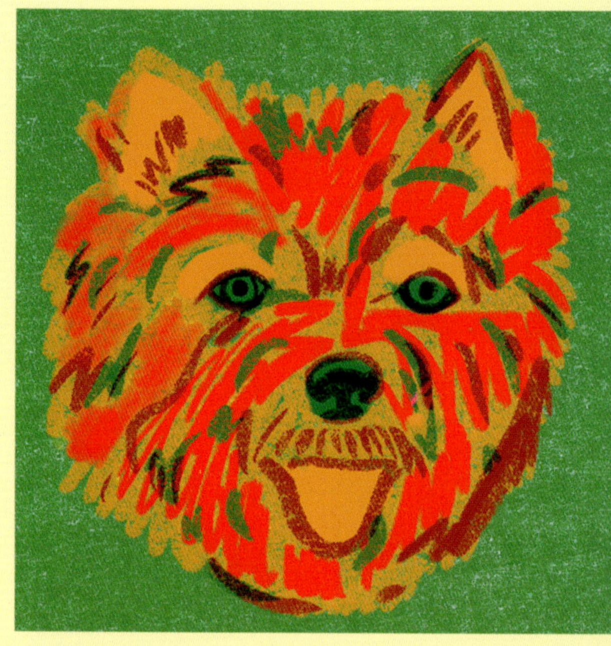

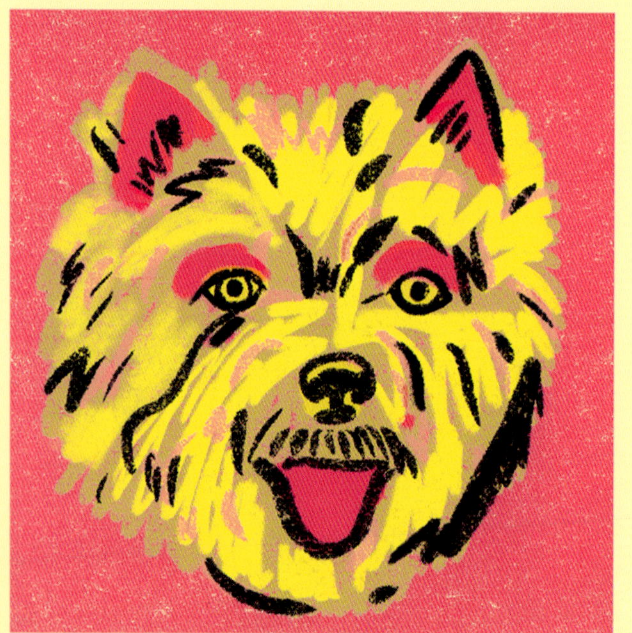

However, this most traditional of genres can feel a little staid. Enter man's best friend, loyal companion and beloved muse of artists the world over. In this book, a selection of playful pooches take centre stage as the subjects of the world's most famous portraits.

Alongside each reimagined artwork is a
breakdown of individual elements that
help us to understand more about the
artist, the sitter and any hidden
meanings within the work.

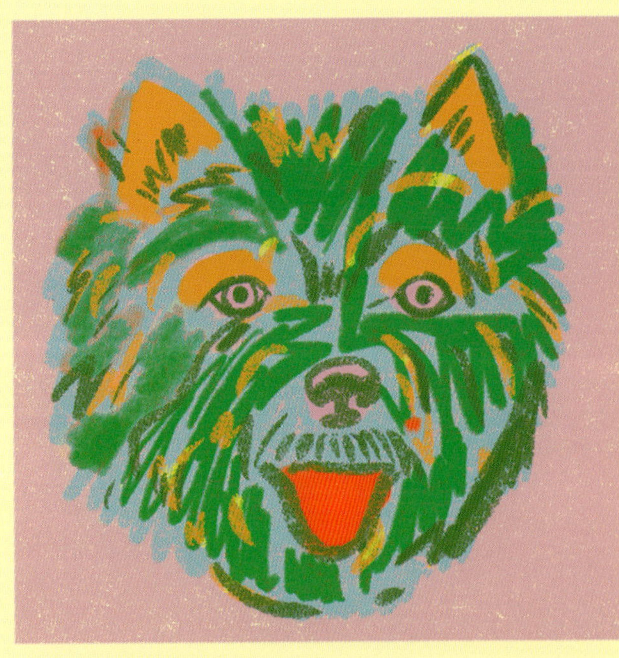

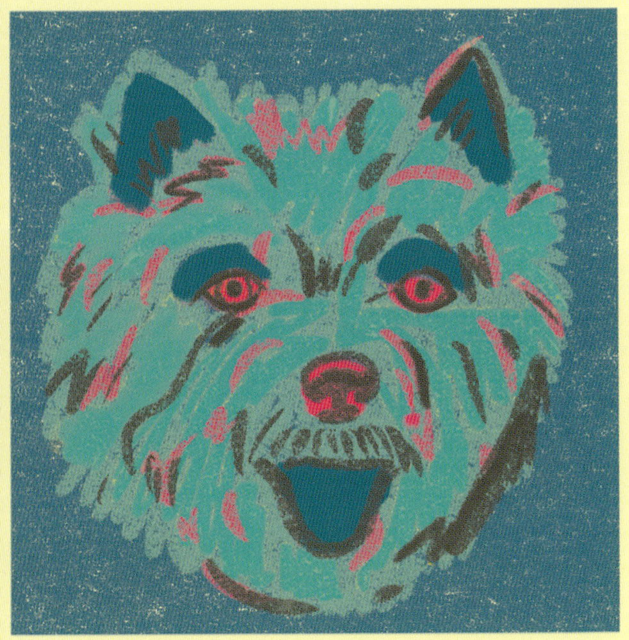

Discover fascinating information about
these most recognizable pieces, then turn
to the back of the book for a helpful
timeline of the artists featured.

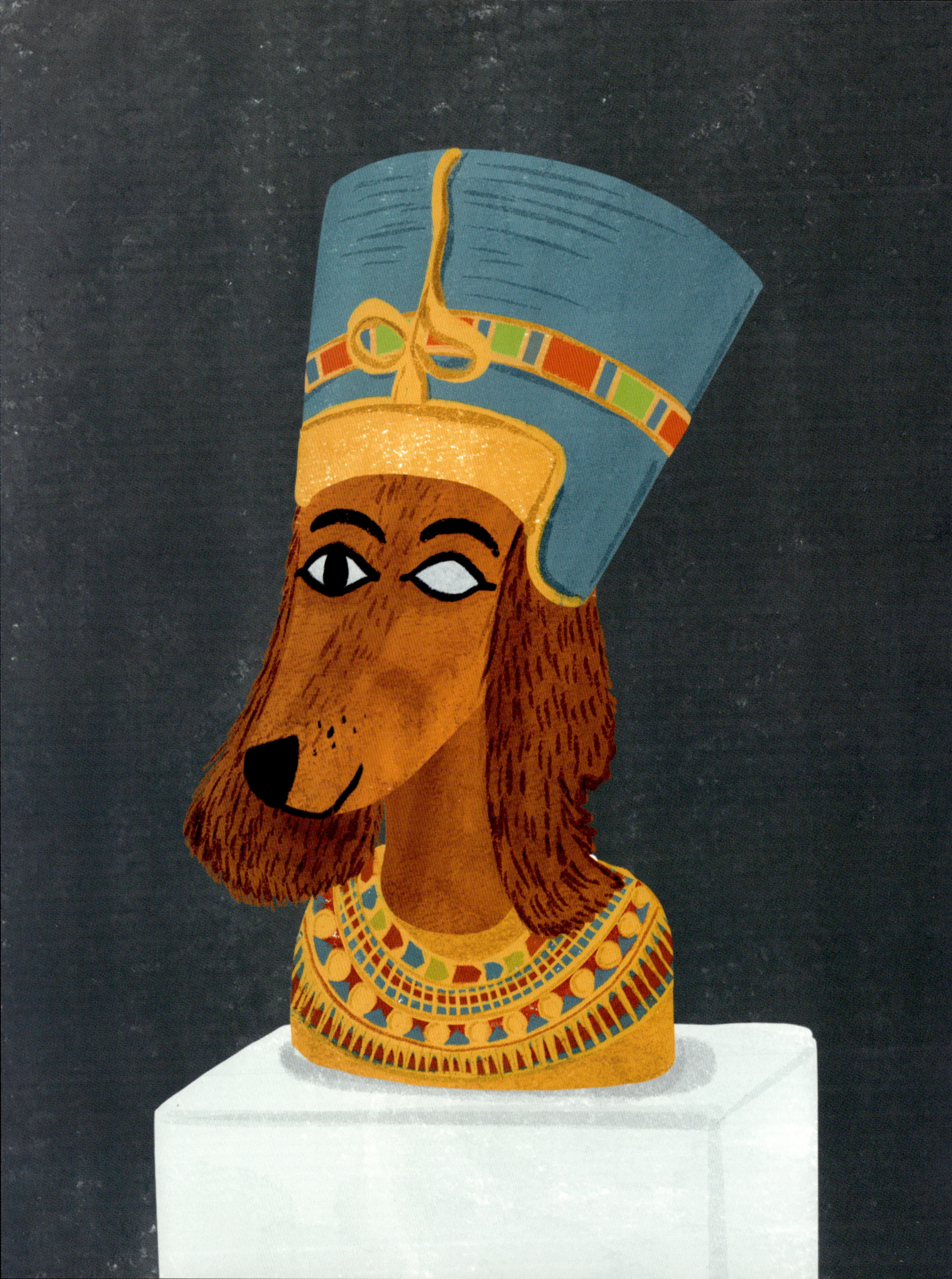

THE BUST OF NEFERTITI BY THUTMOSE

One of the oldest and most historically significant portraits in existence, this stylized yet lifelike rendering of the queen of Egypt, wife of King Akhenaten, is thought to have been created around 1340 BCE. One of the most recognizable artefacts from ancient Egypt, the bust was discovered in the workshop of Thutmose, a court sculptor who created three-dimensional likenesses of the royal family. Created with masterful precision and vibrant hues, it is thought to be a realistic portrayal of the famous queen, whose name translates as 'beautiful woman'.

But who was Queen Nefertiti? An iconic figure in ancient history, Nefertiti is regarded as a strong, independent woman. Some historians believe she acted as co-ruler rather than simply as consort to the king, and was also considered a living fertility goddess and icon of feminine beauty.

This most well known of ancient artworks has stood the test of time. Its rarity (busts were not a common feature of ancient Egyptian art because it was considered vital that representations were complete and intact) paired with its almost immaculate condition mean that it remains one of the most important and fascinating historical works of art in existence.

A MODEL PORTRAIT?

Since its discovery by Egyptologist Ludwig Borchardt in 1912, the bust is generally accepted to have been intended as a sculptor's model, rather than a fully fledged artwork in its own right. Some historians dispute this, arguing that a model would not have the same level of finish. Despite investigations, evidence has proved inconclusive.

TRADITIONAL SHADES

The paints used for the bust kept to the well-known spectrum of ancient Egyptian pigments. These included red ochre, yellow orpiment, green frit, carbon black and 'Egyptian blue'. A combination of these hues was applied to create a realistic skin tone.

The vibrant colours are one of the main reasons the bust is considered extraordinary, even more so considering how well they have been preserved.

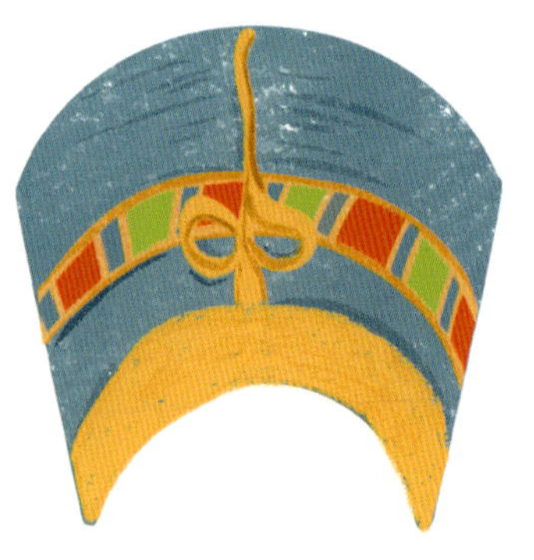

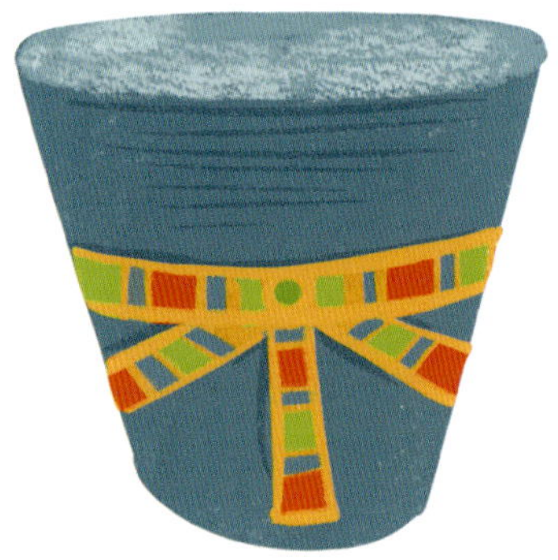

CAP CROWN

Nefertiti wears a characteristic blue crown with a gold diadem band looped aound it. Known as the 'Nefertiti cap crown', it signifies both the power and the elegance of the wearer.

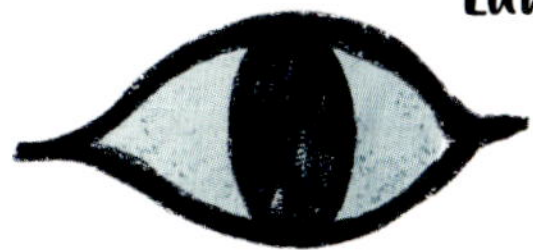

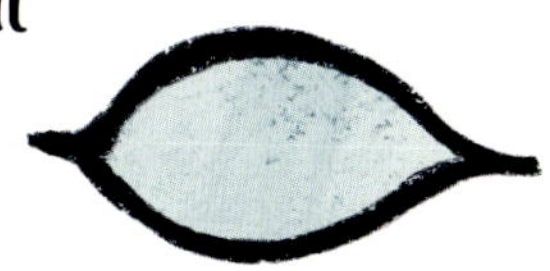

WINGED EYES

The 'cat eye' look can be traced back
to ancient Egypt – kohl eyeliner,
combined with rouge and green
malachite 'eyeshadow', were
common embellishments.

MISSING EYE

The missing left eye is thought to
have been left purposely incomplete
by the artist – backed up by modern
research that found no trace of
inlay, glazing or paint.

JEWELLED NECKPIECE

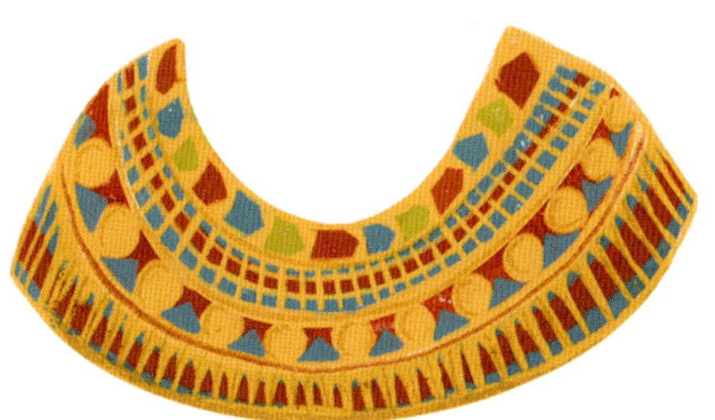

The Usekh, or Wesekh, is a type of broad
collar or necklace, recognizable because of
its presence in many images of the ancient
Egyptian elite. Both men and women were
depicted wearing this jewellery.

LIMESTONE AND STUCCO

The core of the bust is limestone,
over which a layer of stucco was
applied afterwards, before being
finished with paint.

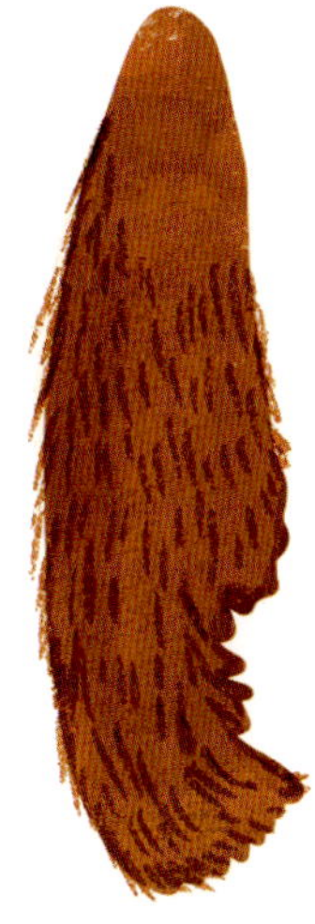

DAMAGED EAR

As opposed to the
smoother right ear,
Nefertiti's left ear ends
roughly. This is thought
to be due to damage,
rather than an artistic
decision to leave
it unfinished.

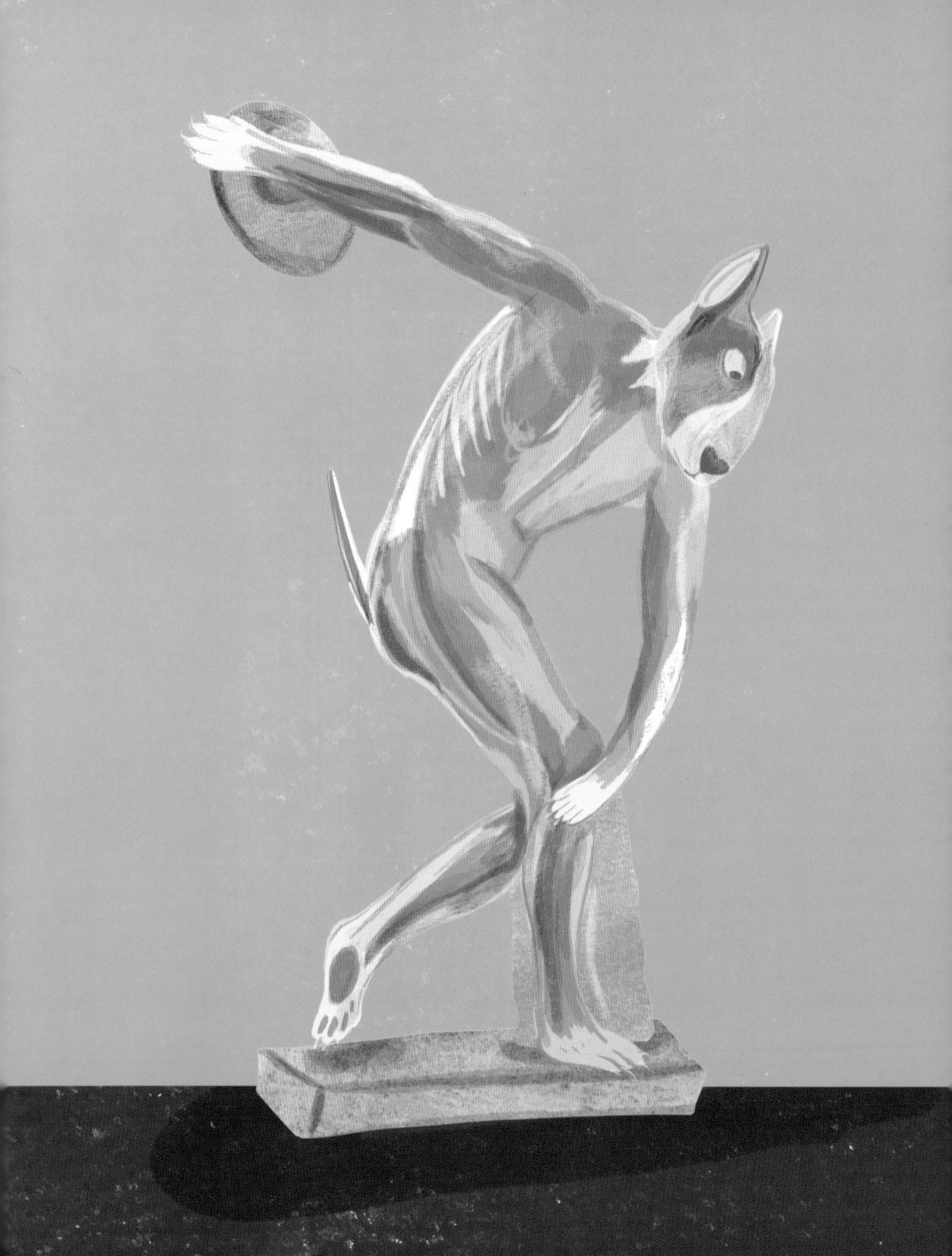

DISCOBOLUS BY MYRON

The world's oldest action figure, the original *Discobolus*, by Myron, dates from around 450 BCE, and depicts a youthful ancient Greek athlete in a dynamic and powerful pose, poised to release a discus. The sculpture symbolizes the 'body beautiful' and is celebrated for its anatomical accuracy. It has become an important emblem of the ancient Greeks.

As well as acting as a snapshot of the Greek ideals of symmetry, proportion and the pursuit of excellence, the *Discobolus* also shows where art and physicality converged in ancient Greek culture. Athleticism was seen to be as vital as intellectual achievement, and this display of physical prowess immortalizes the perfect form that athletes still strive for to this day.

This version, the *Townley Discobolus*, is one of several Roman copies of the original bronze, remade in marble. Influencing countless artists and sculptors throughout history, the *Discobolus* remains a timeless celebration of human achievement and is testament to the enduring legacy of ancient Greek art.

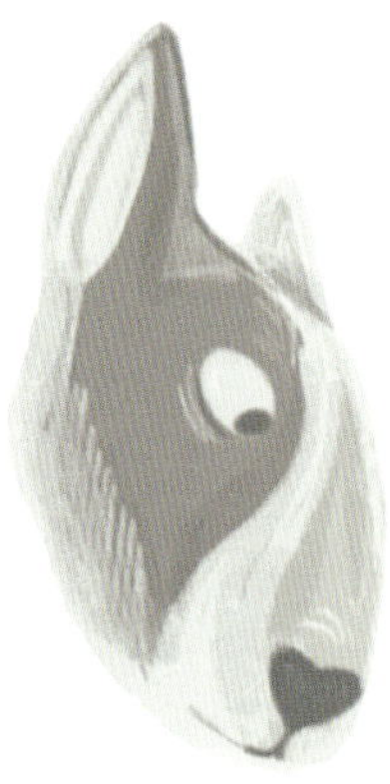

KEEP YOUR HEAD UP

The original bronze *Discobolus* had the head turned to look back at the discus. The Townley version was found with the head missing and was then incorrectly restored.

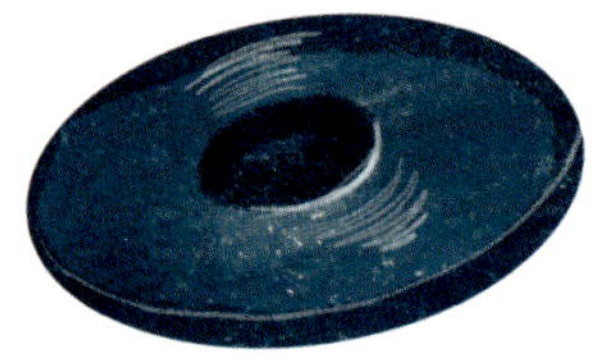

SPORTING PROWESS

Why a discus-thrower? Well, they have historically been admired for their proportion, harmony, rhythm and balance.

"Myron, who almost captured the souls of men and animals in his bronzes ."

Petronius

OLYMPIC FAME

Such is the importance of the statue that it has become an iconic image of the Olympics, and was pictured on the official poster for the games in 1948.

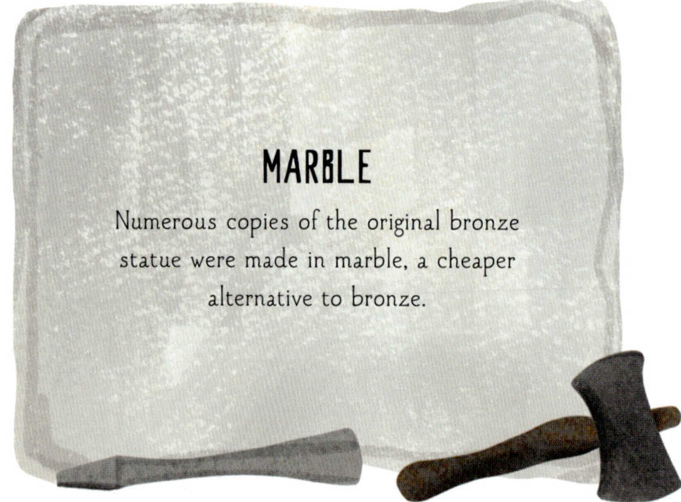

MARBLE

Numerous copies of the original bronze statue were made in marble, a cheaper alternative to bronze.

THE TOWNLEY DISCOBOLUS

It was common in the eighteenth century to restore ancient sculptures without proof that the restored elements actually belonged together: collectors generally valued completeness over authenticity.

The *Townley Discobolus*, as it became known, was discovered in 1791 and purchased by Charles Townley, who took delivery of it in London in 1794. The head of the statue was noted as being in a different position to other copies, but Townley's art dealer, Thomas Jenkins, was adamant that the version he bought was more aesthetically pleasing than Myron's original. Some others were obviously in agreement, as more than one subsequent restoration followed the Townley example rather than the original!

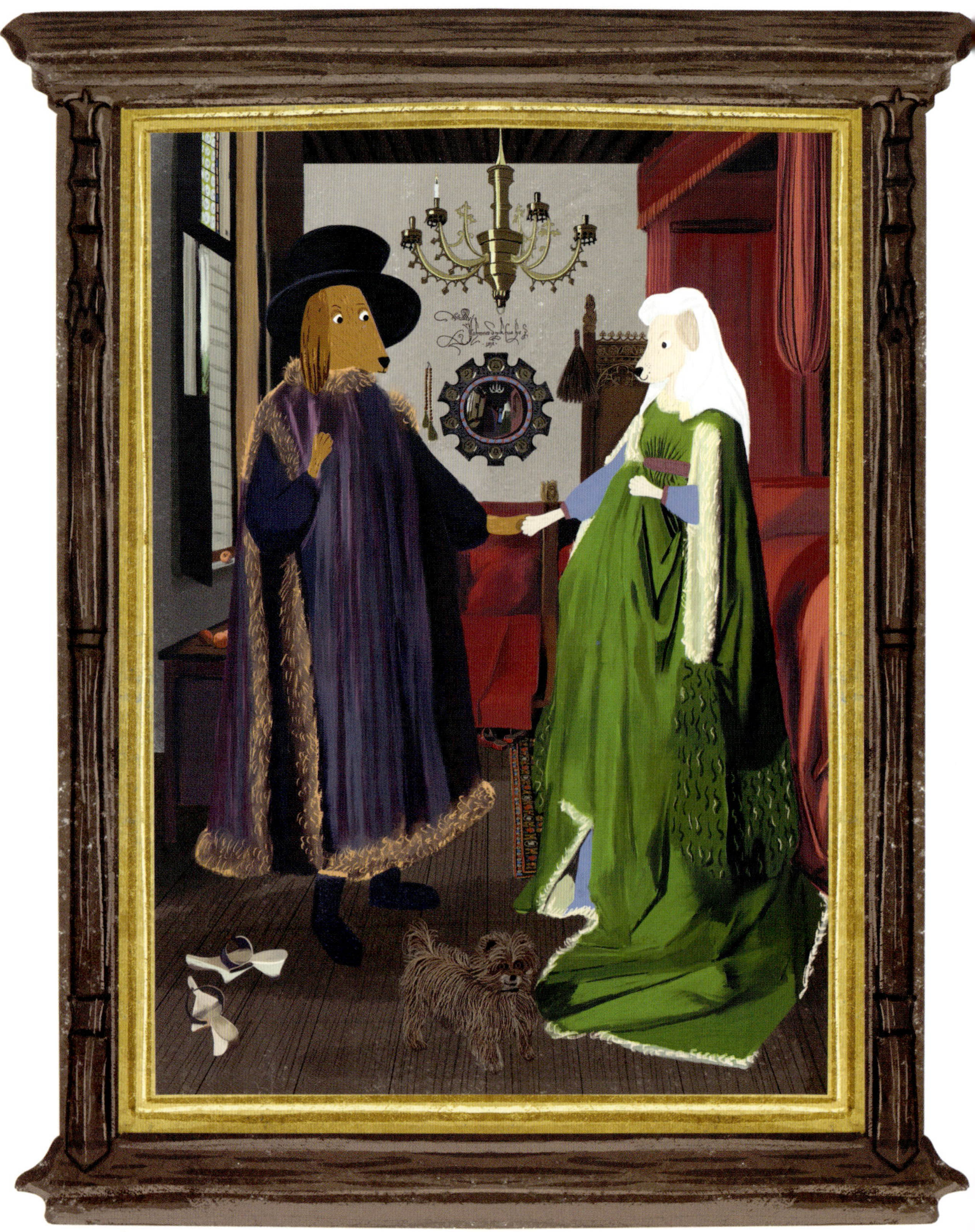

THE ARNOLFINI PORTRAIT BY JAN VAN EYCK

Sometimes referred to as 'the world's most famous wedding painting', the mysteries of this double portrait have given 'paws' for thought for centuries – since it was completed by Belgian artist Jan van Eyck in 1434, in fact. The oldest painting made on an oak panel in oils, *The Arnolfini Portrait* is incredibly detailed and packed with symbolism, some with mysterious, multifaceted meaning.

The initial enigma lies in the subjects themselves. Van Eyck did not make it explicit who the couple were; although they are presumed to have been inspired by Giovanni di Nicolao di Arnolfini and his wife (which explains the name given to the painting). The painting certainly tells the 'tail' of an extremely wealthy couple, but in this portrait many of the background elements have been chosen by the artist to give us clues about the subjects.

The couple stand 'paw-in-paw', and the reflection in the mirror seems to show a figure presiding over a ceremony. However, the wedding theory has long been questioned, and there are equally valid arguments that the portrait was painted in memorial, after Arnolfini's wife died in childbirth in 1433. Whichever way you look at it, this is a painting that has as many interpretations as a dog's soulful stare.

A TECHNICAL REVOLUTION

A notable feature of the painting is the artist's use of his signature method – the application of glazes in incredibly thin layers that give the painting an impressive lustre and textural quality. Known as the 'Flemish technique', it can be seen in many Renaissance paintings, although *The Arnolfini Portrait* is a very early and particularly fine example.

Ultimately, the importance of this painting lies not in its beauty, age, realism, innovative technique or complex symbolism, but in the unique combination of all of these elements, making it one of the most famous works in the history of European art.

> *"Tangible pieces of luminous matter, they confront us with a reconstruction rather than a mere representation of the visible world."*
>
> **Jan van Eyck**

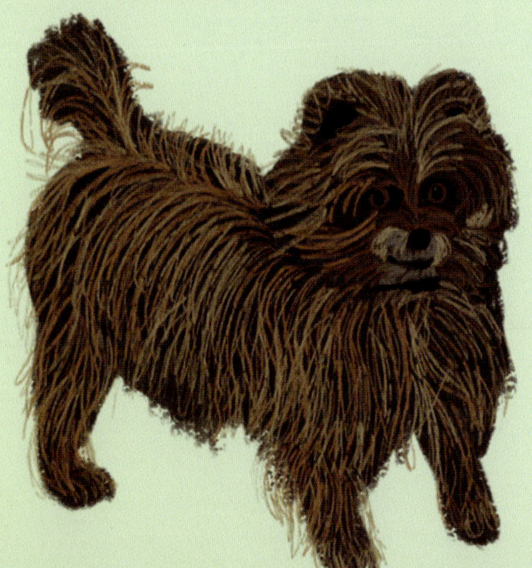

FEELING FRUITY

Along with the couple's fur-lined robes, the oranges denote their wealth – these zesty additions were a rare sight in Belgium at the time.

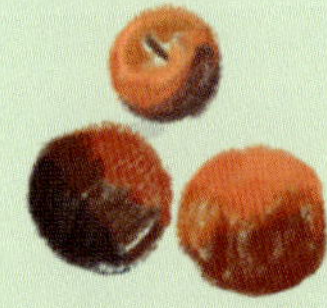

FAITHFUL FRIEND

A furry friend is included at the couple's feet. Dogs were often used in art as a symbolic reference to faithfulness.

Van Eyck applied thin coats of oil glaze in translucent layers, creating the rich tones that give the painting luminosity.

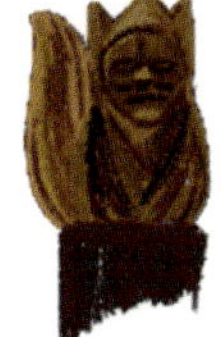

ON THE DOTTED LINE

The prominence and unusual form of the signature, which reads "Jan van Eyck was here 1434", is one of many unclear elements in the painting. The positioning on the wall makes it look more like the signature on a piece of paper than an artist's calling card.

CHAIR CARVING

This carved grotesque, pictured close to the female figure, could have been used to hauntingly prophesize her death, or perhaps signify wealth.

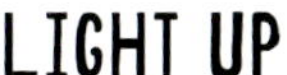

WOODEN CLOGS

The wooden clogs were painted by van Eyck with incredible detail. The finish is so realistic, it almost looks as though you could reach out and touch them.

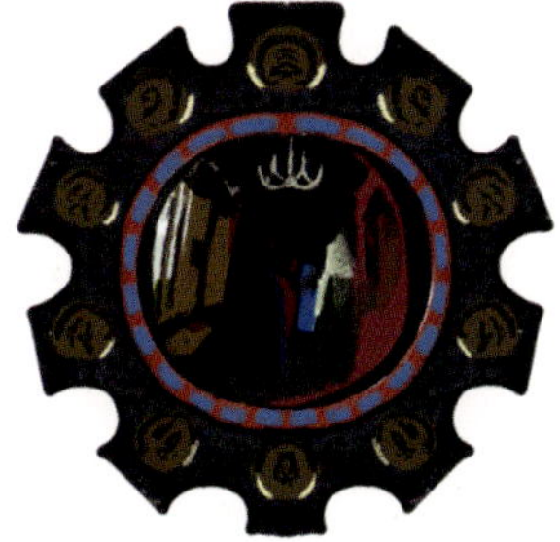

MIRROR, MIRROR

The reflection shows two more figures, giving the impression that a ceremony of some sort is taking place. However, some say that the figures are meant to represent the artist and the viewer.

LIGHT UP

The brass chandelier, with its single lit candle, symbolizes religious presence and was once thought to support the marriage interpretation. However, it could also be intended to signify the death of the person beneath the empty candle holders.

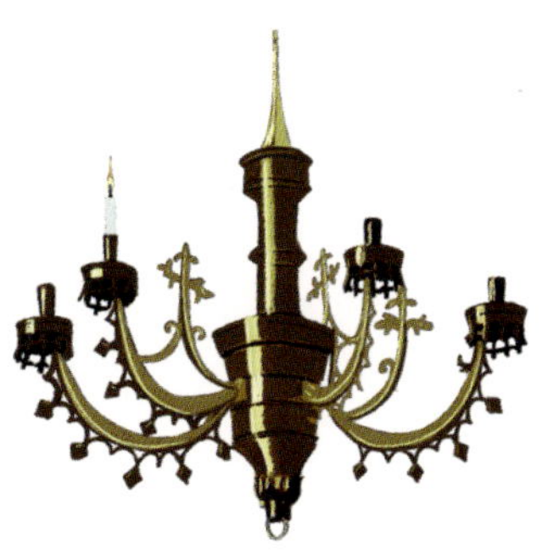

HOLDING HANDS

The clasped 'paws' could be interpreted as representing a contract, perhaps a business deal, with one giving the other the power to act in business. This was common practice at the time.

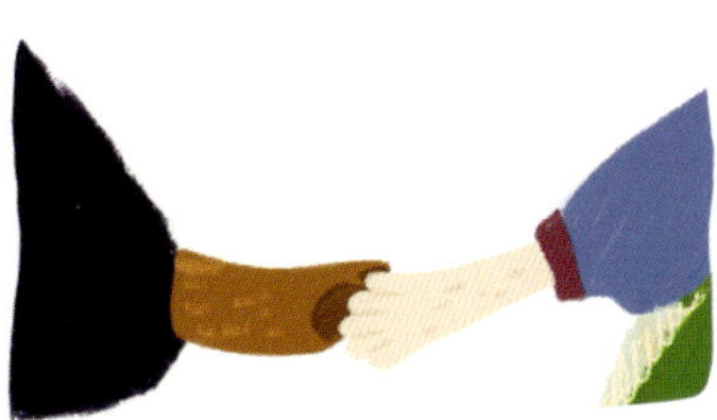

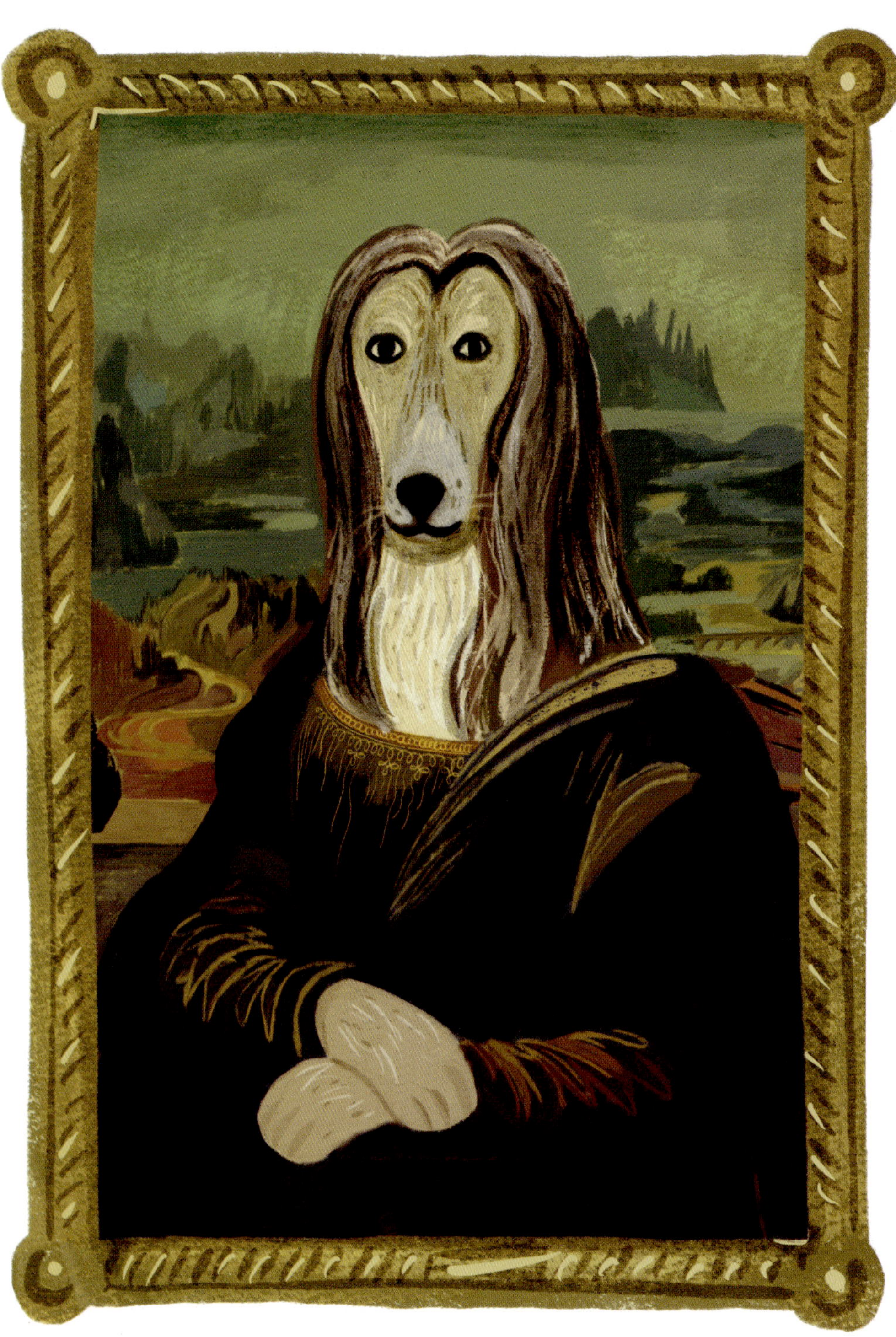

MONA LISA
BY LEONARDO DA VINCI

There can't be many people who couldn't pick the *Mona Lisa* out of a line-up. A master of portrait painting, Leonardo da Vinci created, in the early sixteenth century, an icon of art and innovation that is no less impressive now than it was five centuries ago.

Da Vinci's masterpiece, with its impressively lifelike rendering and enigmatic expression – which seems to change depending on where the viewer's gaze falls – has captured imaginations for centuries. With the identity of the sitter never definitively confirmed, she remains the ultimate subject of art history debates. The *Mona Lisa's* mysterious allure has inspired countless imitations, parodies, some farfetched conspiracy theories and even a heist.

In addition to the *Mona Lisa's* position as a leading icon of pop culture in the modern world, it is clear how this showcase of da Vinci's technical prowess would have influenced his contemporaries in the sixteenth century. It is within this context that the *Mona Lisa* stands out as a work of genius that continues to inspire many other great artists.

A MASTER OF TRADES

Painter, sculptor, architect and engineer, Leonardo da Vinci was a true innovator across many fields. His scientific inquiries, centuries ahead of their time, allowed him to create unprecedented realism in his work. From his study of human anatomy to his development of a mathematical system for determining perspective, he was unique in his combination of science and technical artistry. A true genius!

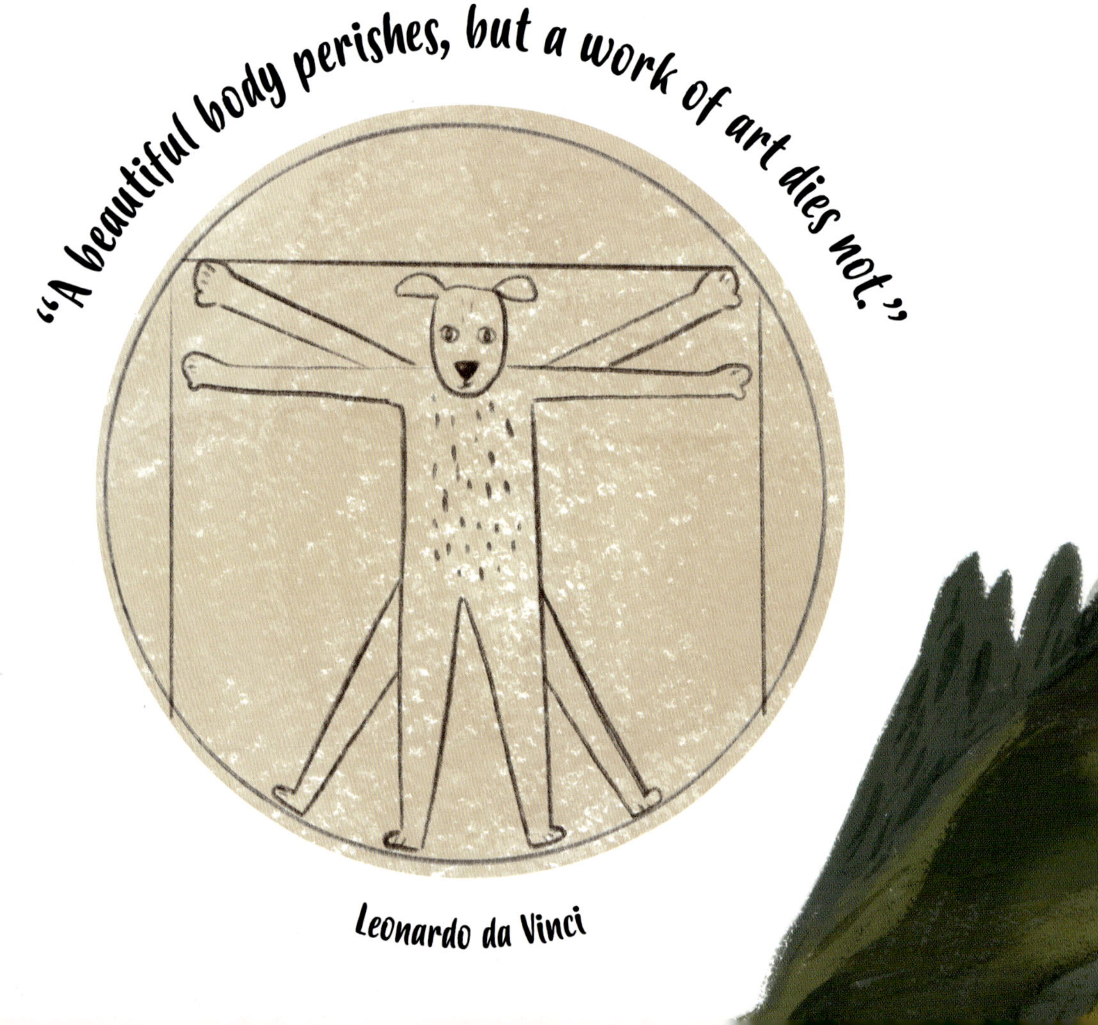

Leonardo da Vinci

SFUMATO TECHNIQUE

Da Vinci was fascinated by the way light falls
on curved surfaces. Mona Lisa's hair and the
luminescence of her skin are created with layers
of thinly applied paint, making her face appear
almost to glow, and giving the painting a magical,
ethereal quality. This technique is known as
sfumato, which means 'to evaporate like smoke'.

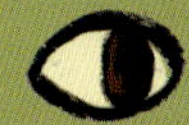 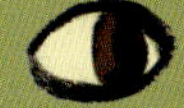

THE EYES HAVE IT

Mona Lisa looks directly out of the
painting, which was an unusual pose for a
woman at the time. The 'Mona Lisa' effect,
which is the perception that the subject's
eyes follow you around the room, has
become a well-documented attribute.

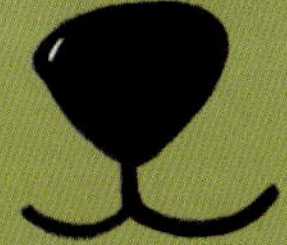

MONA LISA'S SMILE

Whether a result of da Vinci's study of human
anatomy or representative purely of his skill as
a painter, the Mona Lisa's smile is her most
famous feature. While we may never know
the reason for her expression, it does show
da Vinci's deep understanding of how
human emotion can be interpreted.

BLURRED BACKGROUND

Behind the figure, a vast landscape fades away into
the distance, before disappearing in a misty haze.
The contrast between the realism and clarity of the
woman in the foreground and the soft-focus
background lends to the power of the painting. The
location has also been the source of much debate,
with some claiming to recognize landmarks and others
countering that the setting is imaginary.

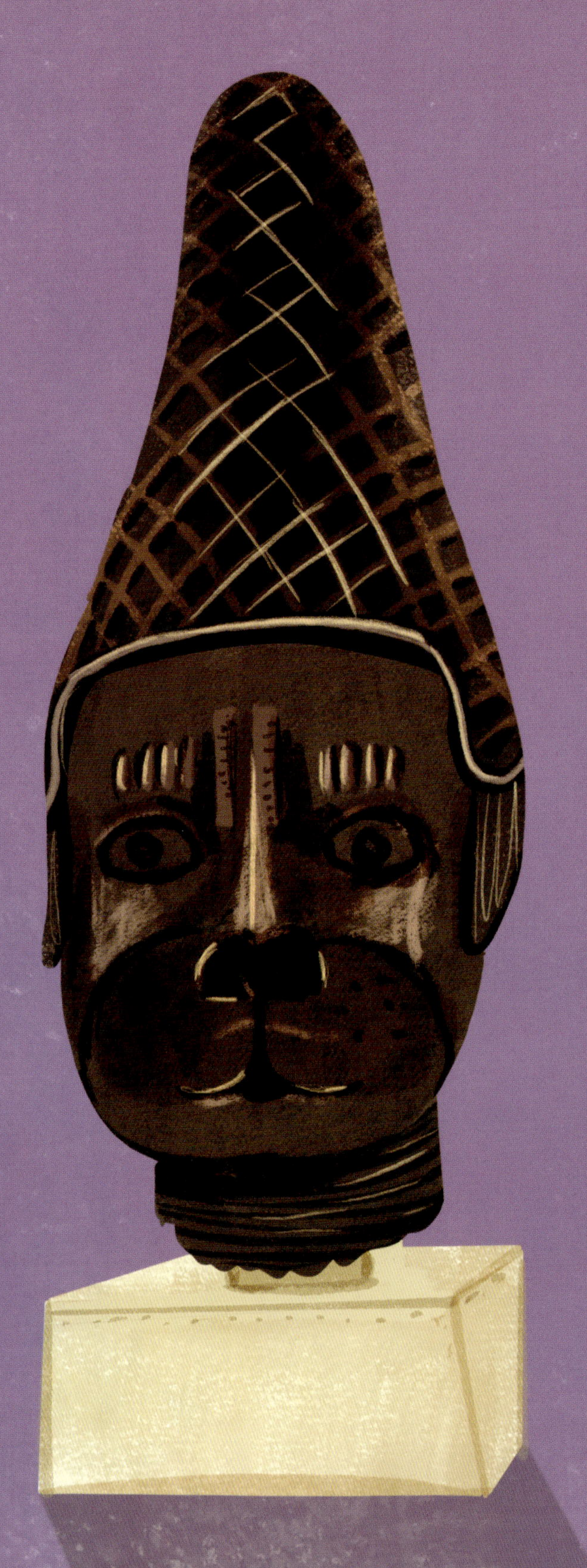

BRONZE HEAD OF QUEEN IDIA

One of a number of cast bronze heads made of the legendary Queen Idia, this commemorative sculpture is an important piece of history from the medieval kingdom of Benin, in West Africa. It was commissioned by her son, Oba Esigie, in the sixteenth century, and created by the imperial guild of brass-casters.

As the first and most famous Queen Mother (or 'Iyoba') of Benin, Queen Idia's role in aiding her son's military and political success was crucial. Renowned as a fearless soldier, she played an instrumental role in her son's successful military campaigns against neighbouring tribes and factions. After her death, he commissioned several commemorative bronzes to honour her achievements and to celebrate her legacy.

The Benin bronzes are considered to be among the finest examples of art made using the 'lost-wax' casting technique. This example has become an important symbol of the cultural heritage of the Edo people, embodying their history, power, and the rich tradition of the Benin Kingdom. The *Bronze Head of Queen Idia* remains an emblem of identity, heritage, and the enduring legacy of African civilizations.

ART IN THE BENIN KINGDOM

The history of art in the Benin Kingdom, dating back to the thirteenth century, is deeply intertwined with its royal court and religion. The Benin Kingdom, located in present-day Nigeria, was renowned for its sophisticated bronze and brass sculptures, particularly the famous 'Benin Bronzes', as they became known.

As well as the bronzes, ivory carvings, intricate plaques, and ceremonial objects adorned the royal palace, narrating the kingdom's history and honouring the Oba's lineage. Art in Benin not only reflected the kingdom's wealth and political structure, but also played a crucial role in religious and ceremonial practices.

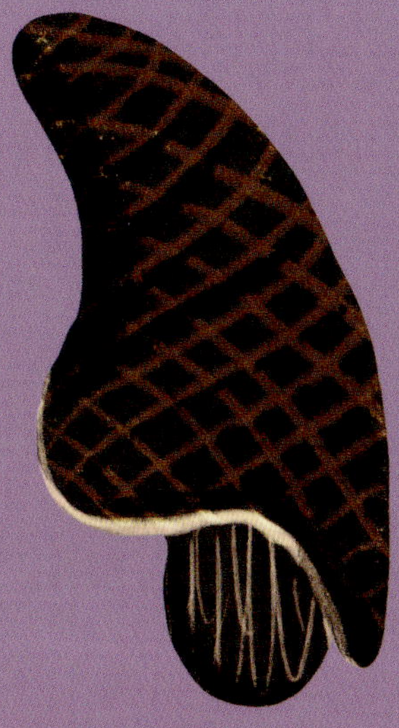

MAKING SHAPES

Queen Idia is thought to have invented this distinctive conical hairstyle, known as 'ukpe-okhue'. Covered with a coral bead headdress, the style was only permitted to be worn by the Queen Mother and was adopted by those who came after her.

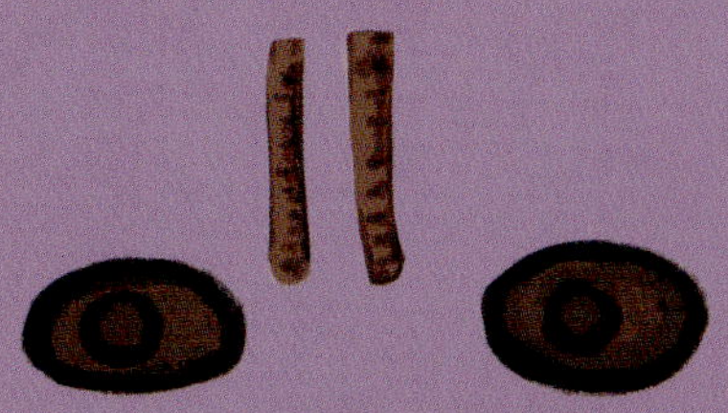

POWERFUL EYES

Symbolizing bravery and strength, two lines of iron inlay between the eyes represent the medicine-filled incisions that were thought to have given Queen Idia her power. The four scarification marks above each eye were used to indicate gender.

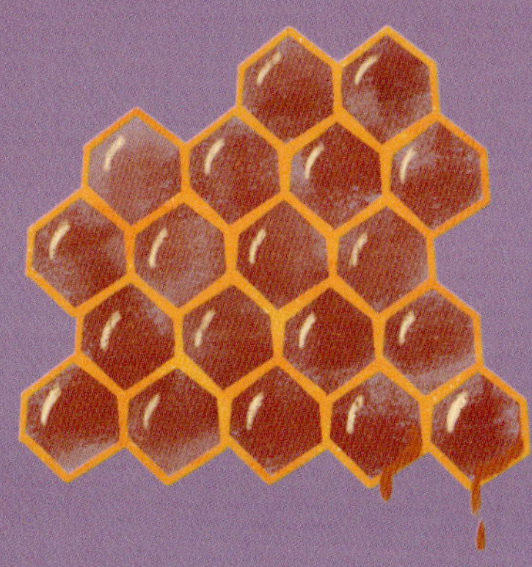

LOST-WAX CASTING

The lost-wax casting technique is an incredibly specialized art form. A model is first made in beeswax, then covered in clay before being heated, to melt away the wax. Molten metal is then poured into the clay mould and left to set before the clay is broken open, leaving behind an intricately detailed bronze model.

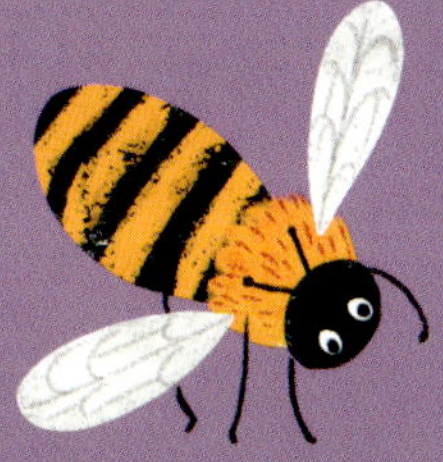

WORKER BEES

The imperial guild of brass-casters was originally founded by Oba Oguola around 1280 CE. He introduced a system whereby artists lived within the palace and worked solely for the Oba. The more powerful the king, the more sophisticated the specialists and, therefore, the sculptures.

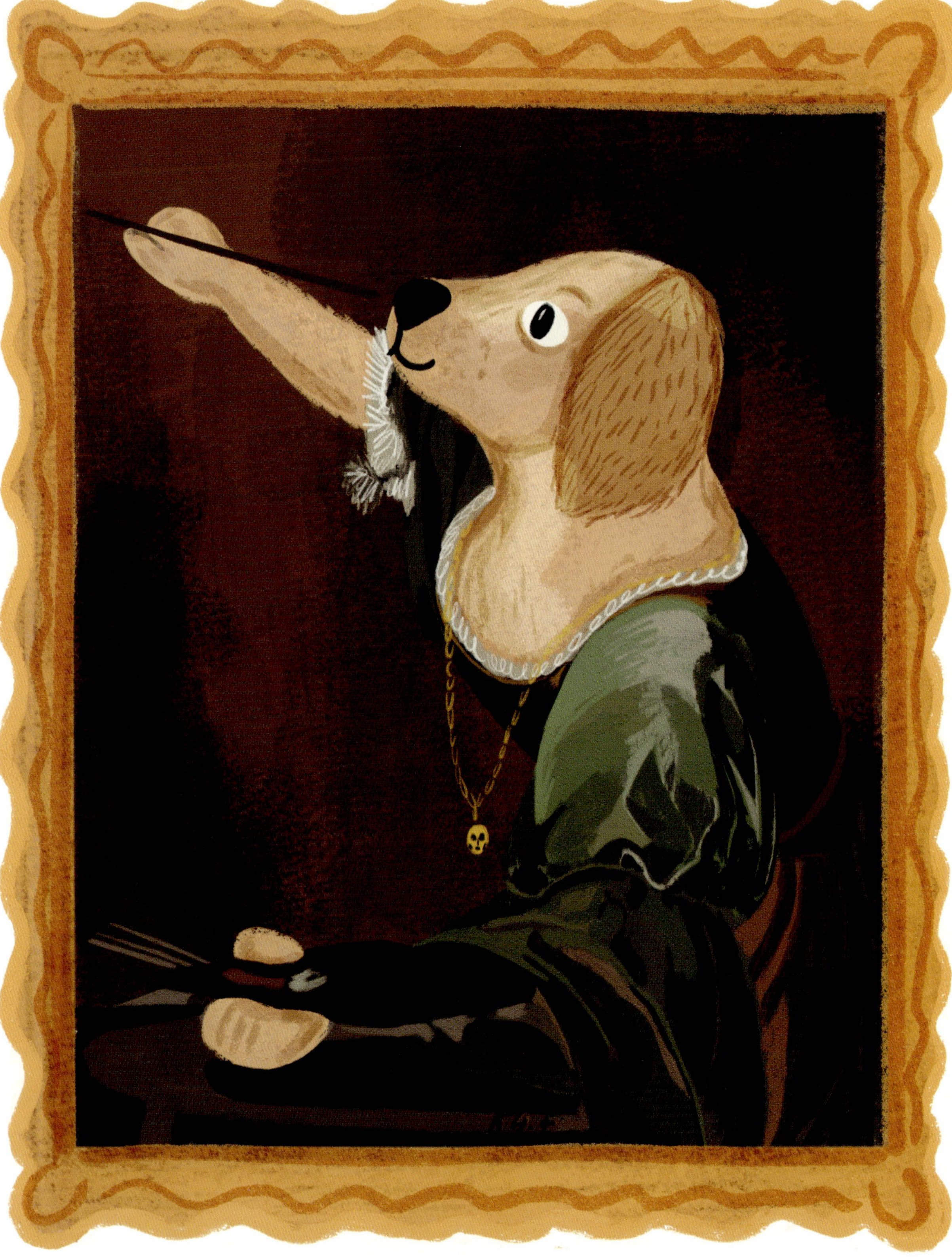

SELF-PORTRAIT BY ARTEMISIA GENTILESCHI

Also known as *Self-Portrait as the Allegory of Painting*, this work by Artemisia Gentileschi, an accomplished seventeenth century painter, is one of the most famous self-portraits by a female artist in history.

Challenging the male-dominated art world with her skill and ingenuity, Gentileschi presents herself in the portrait not merely as an artist, but as 'la pittura', or the female 'personification of painting'. A confident and powerful figure, she holds a paintbrush and palette in her paw, symbolizing her identity as an artist. Her gaze is focused and determined, showing her dedication to her craft. The intensity of her expression shows how deeply she is immersed in her work.

The painting is not only a self-portrait but also a statement of artistic identity and skill. Through her portrayal of herself as the embodiment of painting, Gentileschi asserts her place in the male-dominated art world of the Baroque period and remains to this day a profound commentary on gender, identity, and the role of women in art and society.

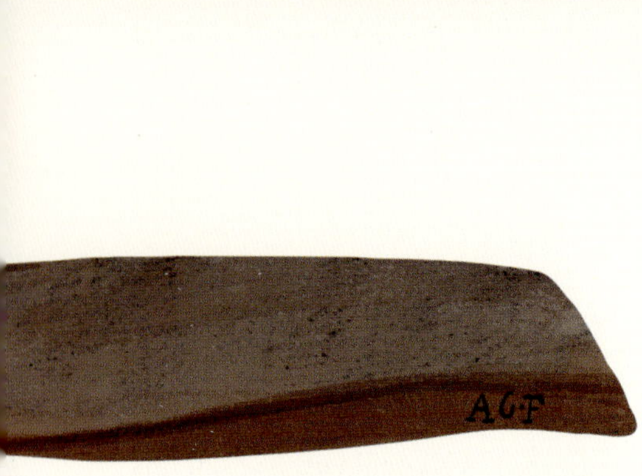

MAKE YOUR MARK

Gentileschi leans on a stone slab
used for grinding pigments, on which is her
signature in large letters – A. G. and F. for
'Fecit' (meaning 'made'). The prominence of the
letters emphasizes the link between the artist
and the physical art of painting.

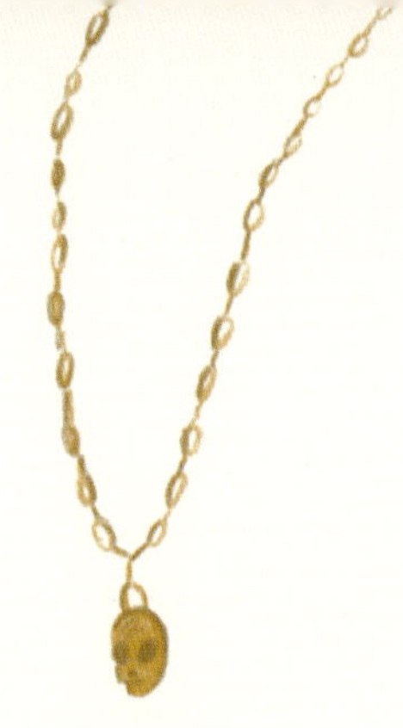

MASK PENDANT AND CHAIN

Along with the draping of the dress she
wears, the gold necklace is a reference to the
description of 'la pittura' in Cesare Ripa's
Iconologia, on which Gentileschi based this
portrait. Ripa's book gave visual representations
to qualities such as vices, virtues and art.

LIGHT VS DARK

The dark backdrop of the piece
contrasts with the illuminated appearance
of the figure, emphasizing the artist's
importance as the central focus. The
luminous impasto effect on the forehead
highlights the power of the
imagination and mind.

MIRROR METHOD, REVERSING REFLECTION

The mechanics of painting a self-portrait from this angle would have been complicated – in order to view her own image, Gentileschi probably set two mirrors at a 45-degree angle. In this way, she would have been able to paint her entire figure without needing to reverse her painting paw.

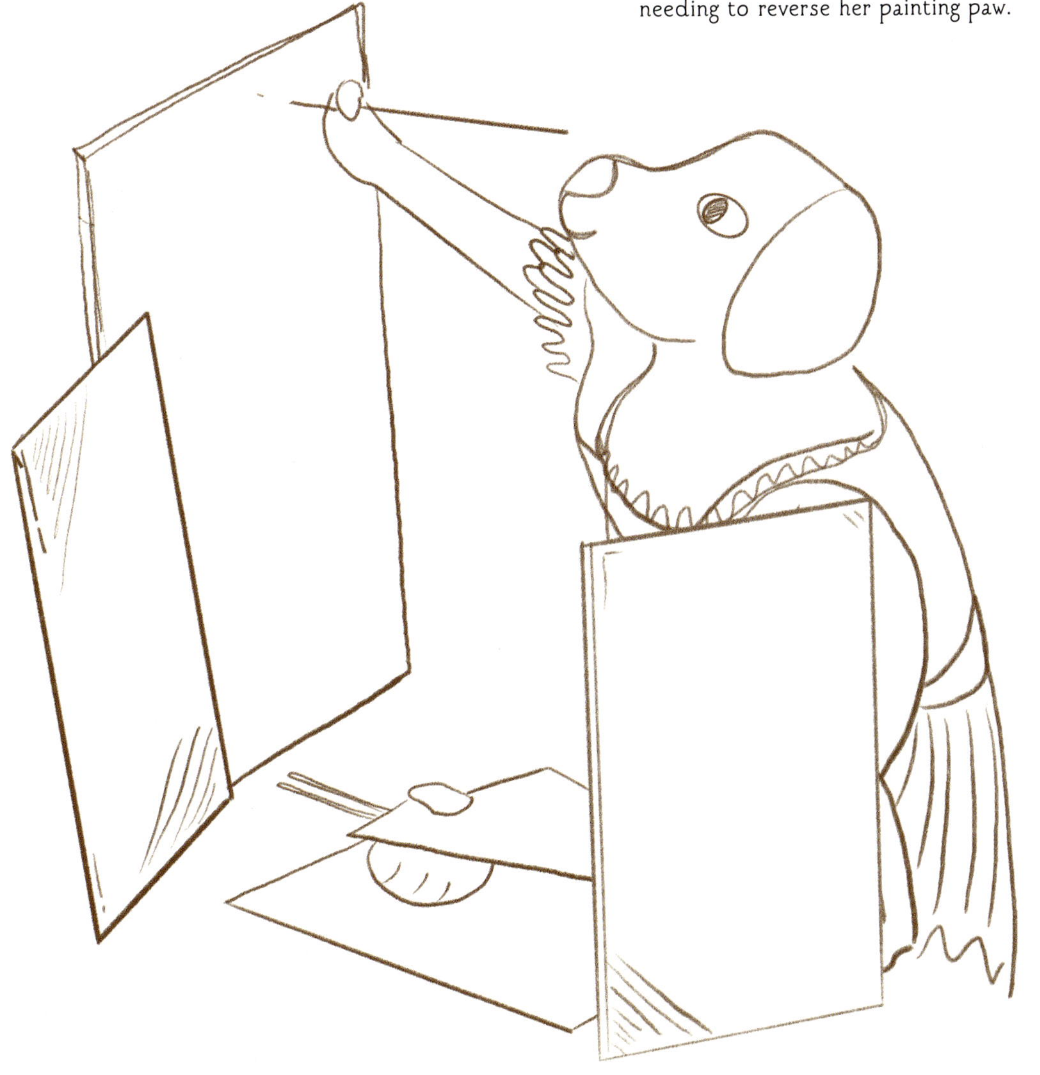

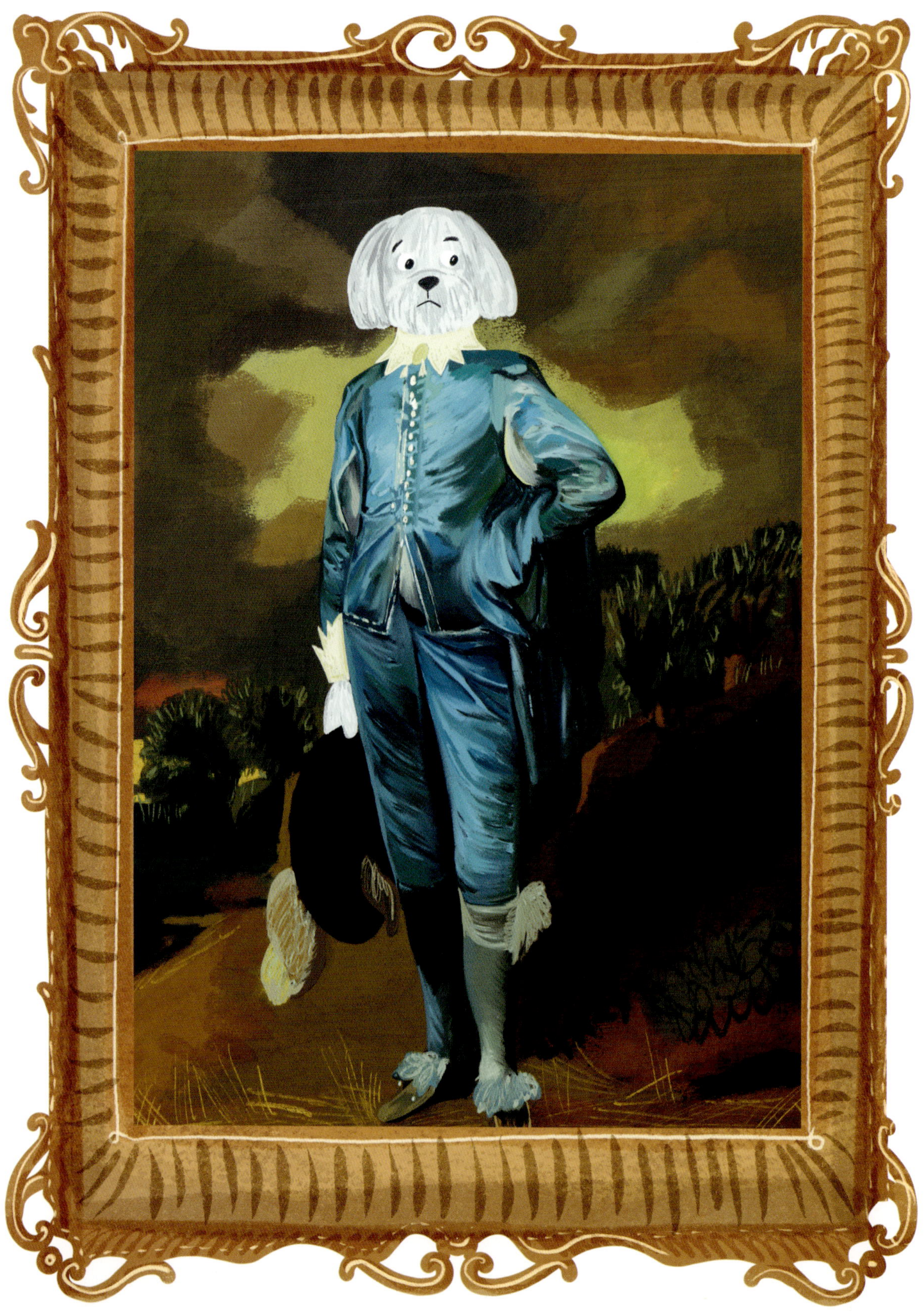

THE BLUE BOY
BY THOMAS GAINSBOROUGH

Once referred to as 'the world's most beautiful picture', *The Blue Boy*'s importance in the canon of portraiture can hardly be overstated. Painted by Thomas Gainsborough around 1770 and initially titled *Portrait of a Young Gentleman*, the painting is a striking example of the genre and demonstrates Gainsborough's mastery of paint pigment, composition and technique.

The painting received immediate critical acclaim, but beyond its technical brilliance, *The Blue Boy* represents the ideal of the English gentleman during the Georgian era, embodying youth, elegance and poise. The identity of the subject was never revealed, but it is thought that Gainsborough probably asked a non-noble adolescent to imitate the pose of the Duke of Buckingham in an Anthony van Dyck painting from 1628, as an homage to his work.

Emulated by artists and revered by collectors, the painting has become a cultural symbol, influencing fashion and popular culture for centuries. *The Blue Boy* remains an enduring symbol of British art and of Gainsborough's lasting legacy.

THE GREAT PRETENDER

Dressing up in and being portrayed in 'van Dyck' costume was not unusual at the time *The Blue Boy* was painted – but with *The Blue Boy*, Gainsborough was also making a statement about his relationship with past artists, and contrasting it with his own contemporary innovations. As well as the obvious similarities in pose, Gainsborough also borrows some techniques from van Dyck's work, as well as the styling of the piece as a whole. In this way, Gainsborough advertised his admiration for the Anglo-Flemish painter, and invited comparison between himself and the master of the genre.

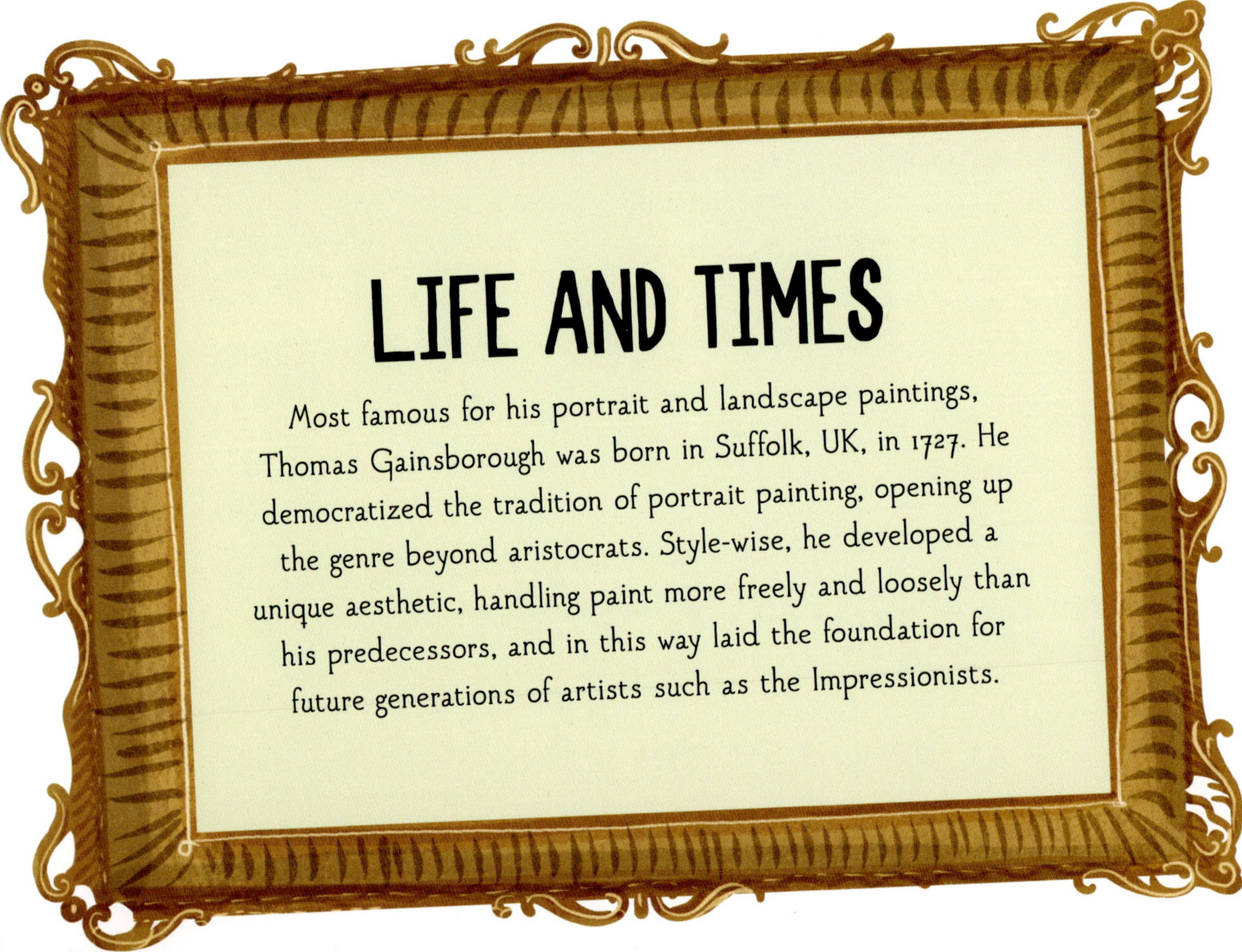

LIFE AND TIMES

Most famous for his portrait and landscape paintings, Thomas Gainsborough was born in Suffolk, UK, in 1727. He democratized the tradition of portrait painting, opening up the genre beyond aristocrats. Style-wise, he developed a unique aesthetic, handling paint more freely and loosely than his predecessors, and in this way laid the foundation for future generations of artists such as the Impressionists.

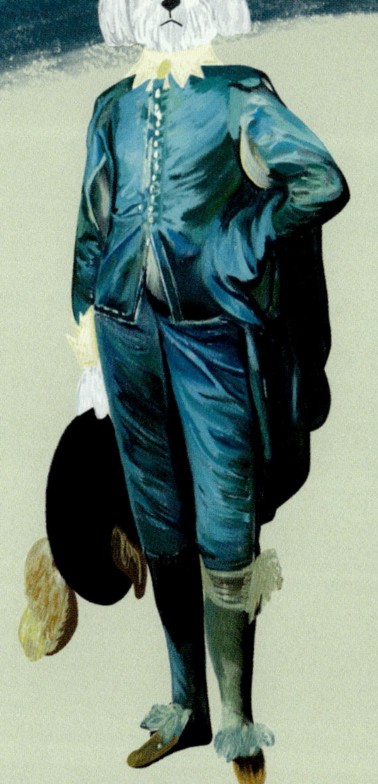

STRIKE A POSE

In 1770, the pose of the 'blue boy' would have been recognized as noble, signalling an exemplary future husband and father. He is standing in an authoritative position known as 'contrapposto' or 'counterpoise', frequently used in classical art. The jutting elbow is a common feature of European portraiture, expressing masculinity.

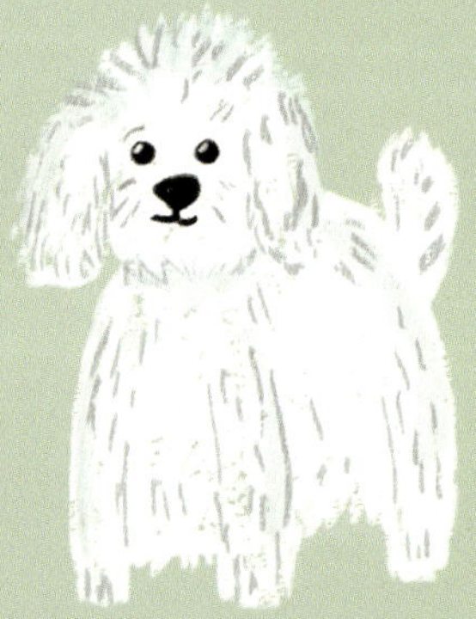

A MISSING PUP

Modern x-rays show that Gainsborough originally painted a small white dog next to the boy, but subsequently painted over it.

MASQUERADE MASTERPIECE

A historical costume study as well as a portrait, Gainsborough had used the same costume in previous portraits, perhaps as a practice run before embarking on the final masterpiece.

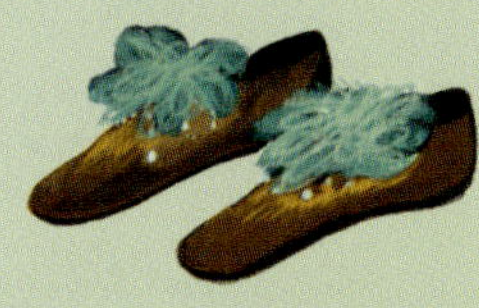

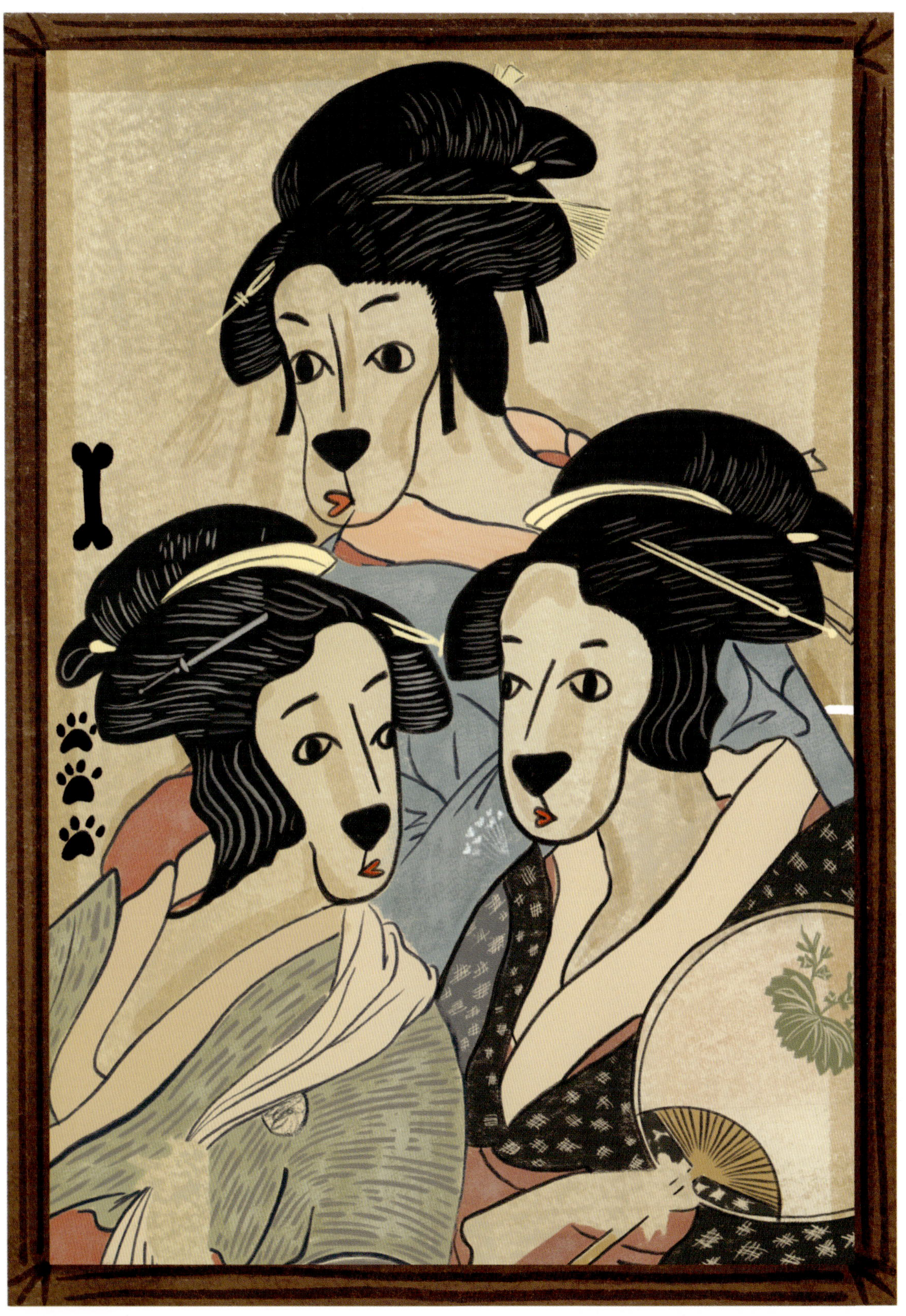

THREE BEAUTIES OF THE PRESENT DAY BY KITAGAWA UTAMARO

Long before Warhol stated that "everybody will be famous for fifteen minutes", Kitagawa Utamaro created the ultimate snapshot of celebrity culture in Edo-period Japan. *Three Beauties of the Present Day* features three of the most famous women of the era – geisha Tomimoto Toyohina and teahouse waitresses Naniwaya Kita and Takashima Hisa. In doing so, he highlighted the cultural and social importance of courtesans at the time, while simultaneously showcasing his exceptional skill in capturing female beauty and emotions.

Notable for his technique as well as his choice of subjects, Utamaro's combination of delicate lines and subtle tones brought a new level of sophistication to *ukiyo-e* style. His ability to capture the individuality and elegance of his subjects, while combining the figures in a perfectly balanced composition, is testament to his skill.

A timeless masterpiece, this portrait provides insight into the aesthetics and society of eighteenth-century Japan. Utamaro's portraits of women caught the attention of many artists, most notably Vincent van Gogh, Claude Monet and Edgar Degas, and the popularity of his work played an important role in increasing appreciation and understanding of *ukiyo-e* art worldwide.

Utamaro's combination of delicate lines and subtle tones brought a whole new sophistication to ukiyo-e style.

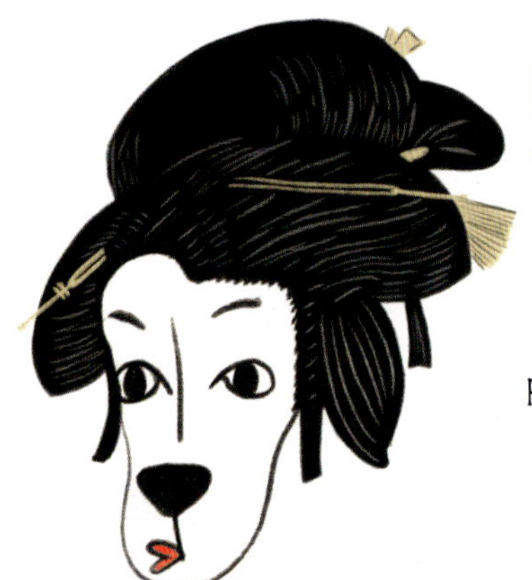

ELABORATE HAIRSTYLES

The three women portrayed in this artwork exude elegance and grace with their intricate hairstyles and traditional attire. Their hairstyles provide an insight into the fashions and beauty standards of the time.

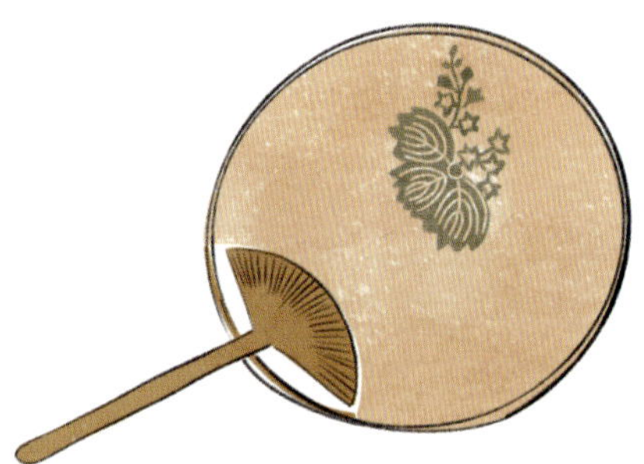

FAMILY CREST

Each woman is wearing a family crest, placed on her kimono or fan, allowing us to identify them.

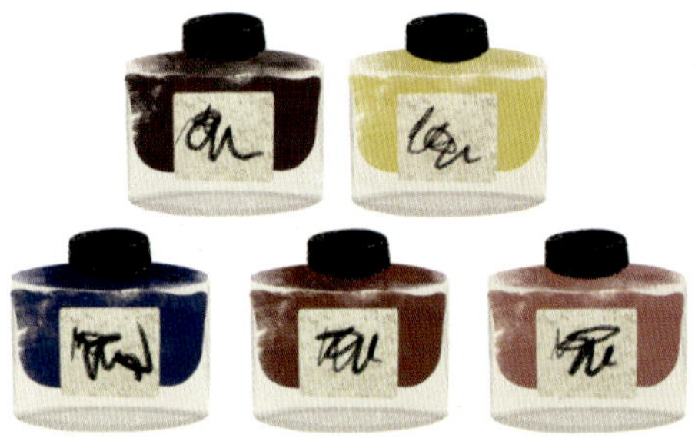

INKS

The inks that Utamaro used for his woodblock prints were plant-based, which means that they are prone to fading and discoloration. Fortunately, the multiple prints allowed by the *ukiyo-e* technique make it possible to piece together a good impression of what the original works would have looked like.

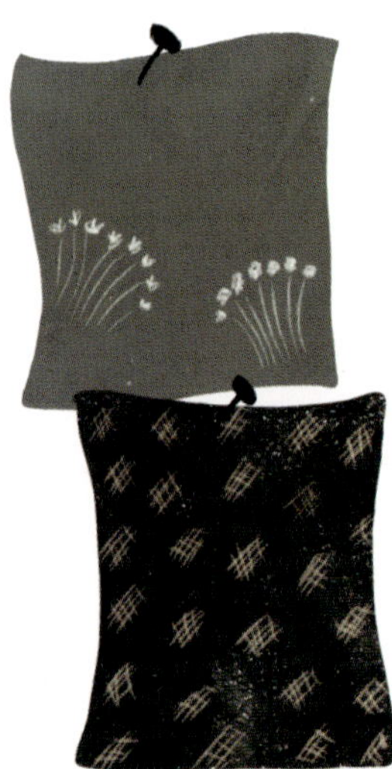

KIMONO PRINTS

Each subject has their own unique style, reflecting different aspects of beauty celebrated during the Kwansei period. The subtle variations may reflect differences in the personalities and statuses of the three women.

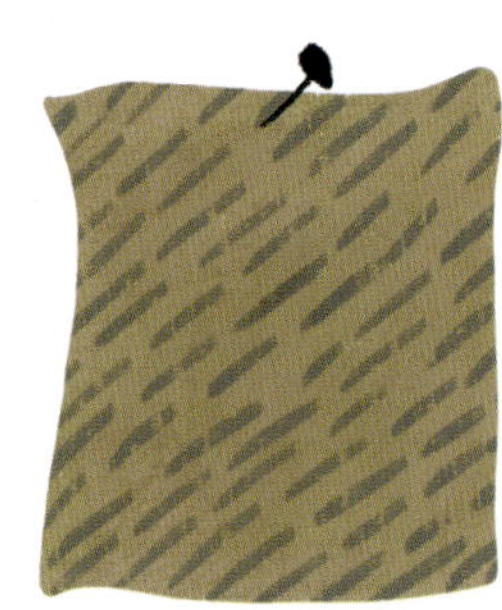

WHAT IS UKIYO-E?

Ukiyo-e is a style of woodblock printing that is uniquely and authentically Japanese. The name itself translates as 'pictures of a floating world', referencing the fleeting nature of life that came to be celebrated, rather than feared, in this era. The art flourished in Japan during the Edo period from the seventeenth to the nineteenth centuries, capturing everything from daily life to scenes of fantasy and adventure.

The prints were painstakingly created – the artist would first carve their design into a woodblock, then ink the raised parts, before pressing the block on to the paper in a form of relief printing. Although laborious, the woodblock method meant that large numbers of prints could be created from a single design.

Although extremely popular, the themes, aesthetics and mass-produced nature of *ukiyo-e* meant it was not considered a serious artform in its own right until relatively recently.

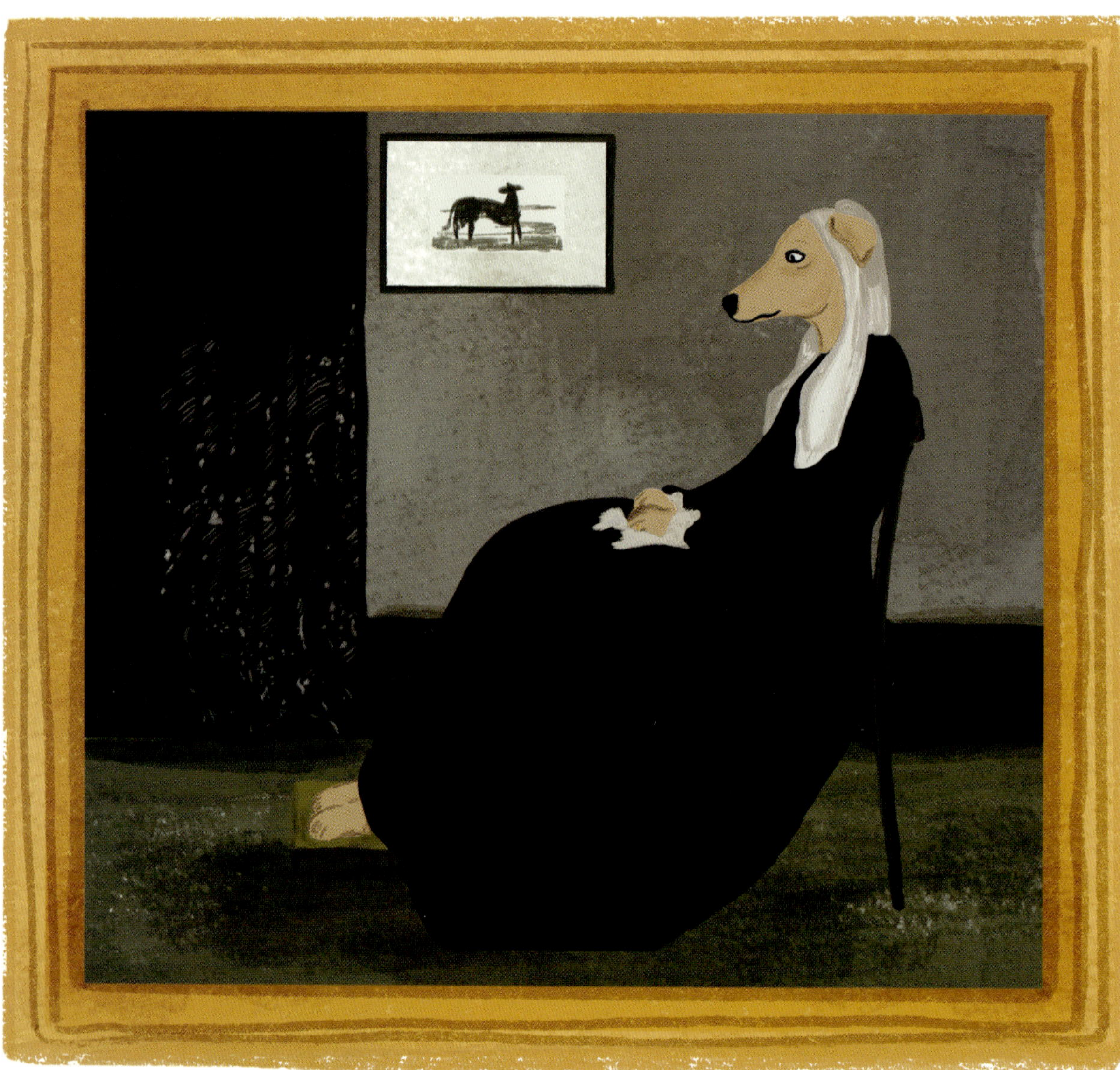

ARRANGEMENT IN GREY AND BLACK NO. 1 BY JAMES MCNEILL WHISTLER

Known as the 'Victorian *Mona Lisa*', this quietly dignified American painting has been said to represent motherhood, parental affection and family values. The woman, the artist's mother, wears Victorian mourning dress, clothed all in black. She sits on a raised platform, the angle meaning the artist is quite literally 'looking up' to the central figure, his mother, the matriarch.

However, given Whistler's profound influence on the Aesthetic movement, such a sentimental reading may be misplaced. Instead, emphasis could be placed on the soft and delicate brushstrokes, restrained use of colour and austere composition that make this portrait a masterpiece of the movement.

Whether Whistler intended the work as a deeply personal portrait or as an aesthetic experiment, it nevertheless affirmed his status as an artist to be reckoned with on both the American and European art stage. Whatever the intent, it remains a timeless painting that resonates with people across generations.

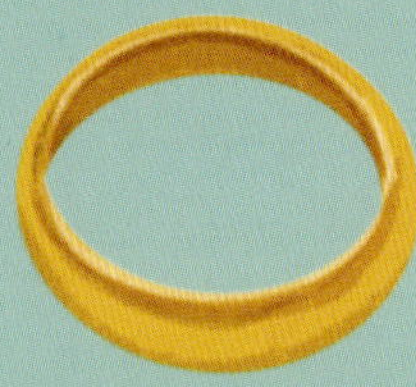

WEDDING BAND

The glimmer of a wedding ring provides a small accent of gold, complementing the gilded frame that Whistler himself designed specially for the painting.

WHITE LACE CAP

A pious woman, shown by her white lace cap, Anna Whistler lived with her son and although it is documented that she struggled to accept his bohemian lifestyle, they cohabited amicably for around a decade.

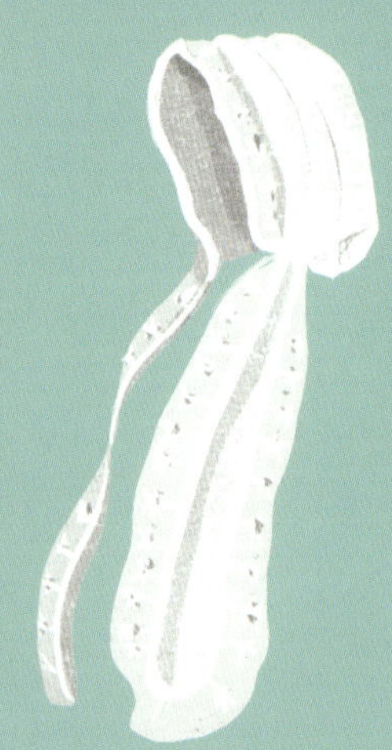

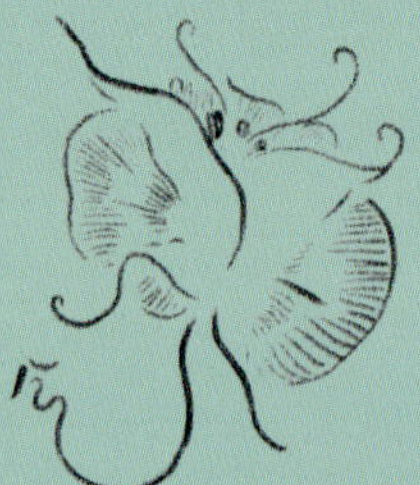

BUTTERFLY SYMBOL

Whistler's signature emblem is a stylistic take on his initials, JW.

SUBDUED PALETTE

The heavily muted palette of greys and blacks, with only the face and paws in fleshy tones, gives a repressed feel to the painting.

MOVEMENT VS AUSTERITY

Despite being inanimate, the curtain has the most dynamic pattern in the painting and works as a point of contrast with the sombre mood of the rest of the piece.

WHAT IS 'AESTHETICISM'?

The central principal of Aestheticism, of which James Whistler was a central figure, was 'art for art's sake'. Rather than serving a wider purpose that was moral, political, or even storytelling, works of Aestheticism were created with a strong emphasis on stimulation of the senses, technique and composition above all else. The suggestion that art should be part of everyday life was central, and the movement embraced decorative crafts as well as more traditional 'fine' art.

Importantly, Aestheticism helped pave the way for movements such as Art Nouveau and blurred the boundaries between art and lifestyle.

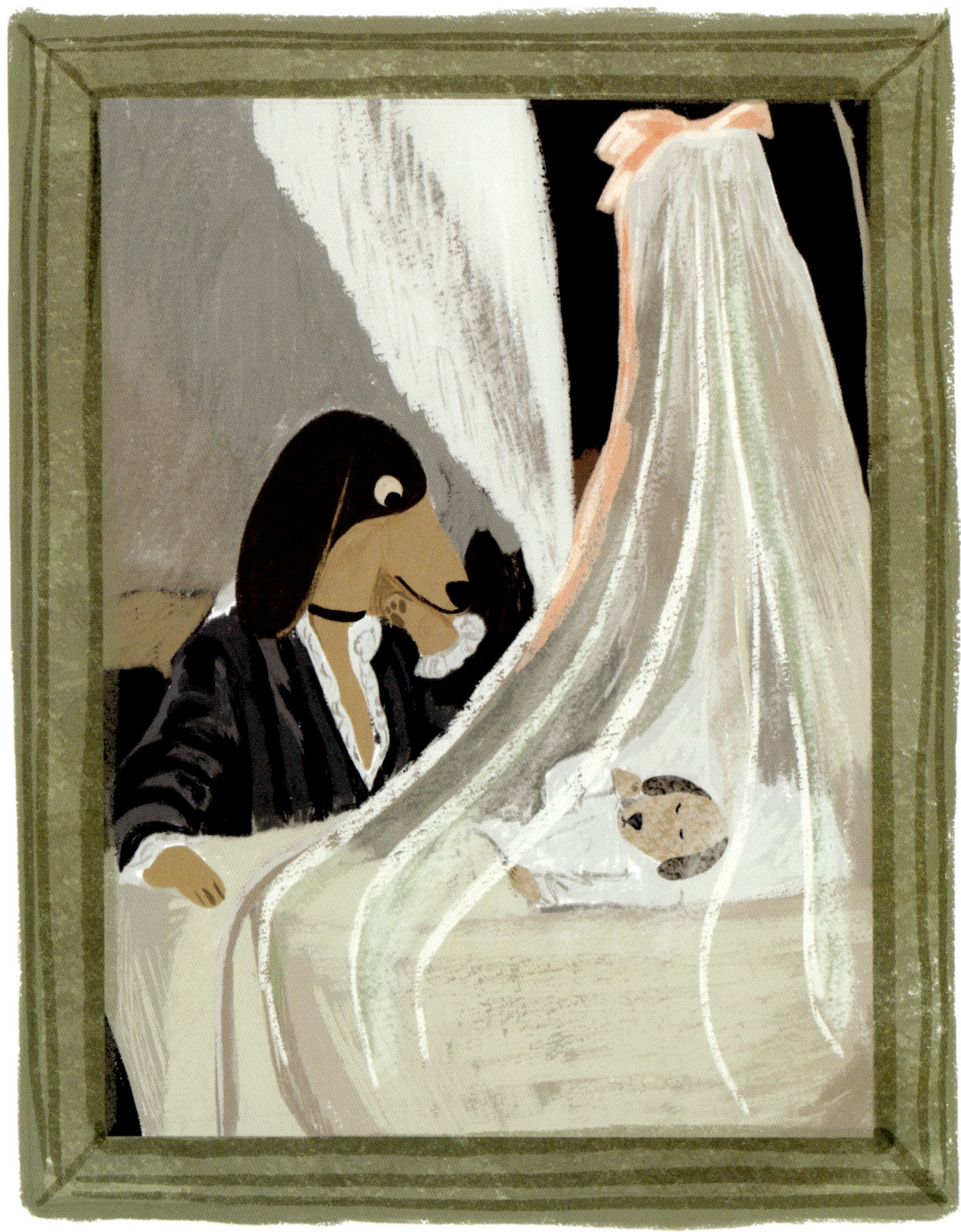

THE CRADLE
BY BERTHE MORISOT

Berthe Morisot's most famous painting is a portrait of her sister, Edma Pontillon, watching over her sleeping daughter. Painted in 1872, it was first exhibited in 1874 at the inaugural Impressionist exhibition. This painting did not go down well at the show, perhaps in part due to the difference in subject matter from other, more traditionally Impressionist pieces.

The Cradle marked the introduction to the theme of motherhood in Morisot's art. Her work on the subject draws predominantly on psychological aspects, aiming to capture the challenges and introspections of motherhood. Morisot rarely painted men, instead focusing on women and children in domestic scenes of everyday life.

Morisot's work, although recognized during her lifetime, was overshadowed by the work of other Impressionsists such as Pierre-Auguste Renoir, Claude Monet or Édouard Manet. Whether this was because critics preferred works painted 'en plein air' – which means 'outside' – to the domestic scenes Morisot favoured, it nevertheless cannot detract from the elegance and grace captured in this portrait.

CRADLE CANOPY

The translucent fabric around
the cradle, appearing in variable
densities, shows off Morisot's
delicate use of light.

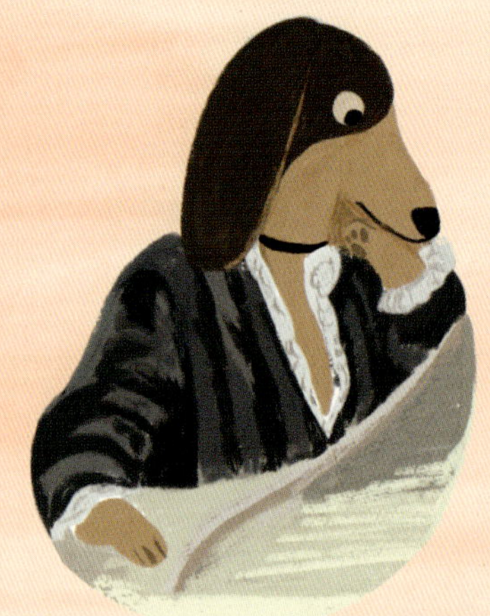

'PAWS' FOR THOUGHT

Pointing in different directions, the
position of the 'paws' represents the pull of
motherhood versus the lure of the art world.
The subject had herself begun an artistic
career, which came to an end when she
married and started a family.

PUPPY LOVE

A focus on motherhood was both
a key feature of Morisot's work
and also, arguably, the reason
Morisot achieved less acclaim than
her fellow Impressionists. At a time
when gender-based discrimination
was common, it is clear how this
theme may have had a detrimental
effect on her success.

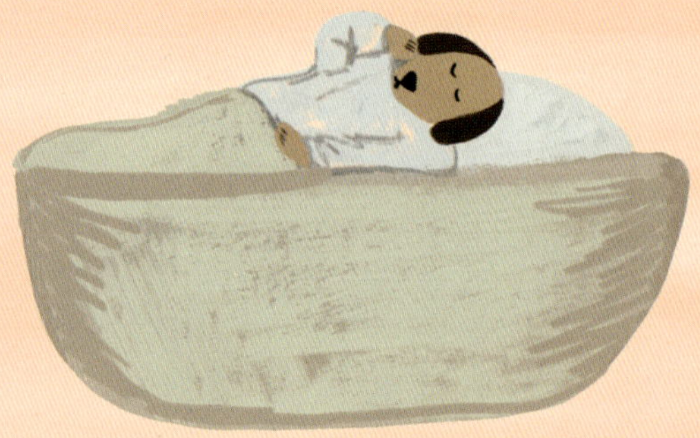

*"No-one represents Impressionism with more refined
talent or with more authority than Morisot."*
Gustave Geffroy

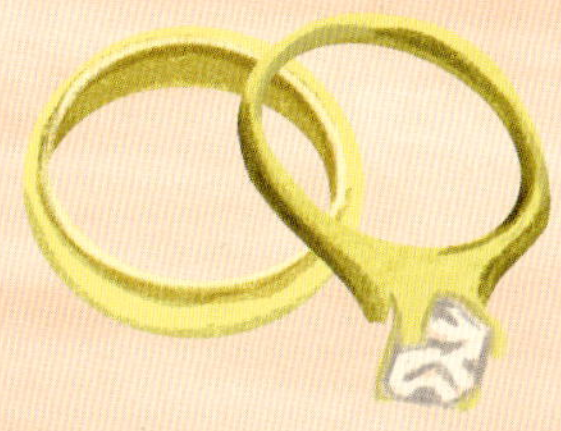

SUBVERTING STEREOTYPES

For many years, Morisot had no interest in marriage, instead devoting herself to her work. When she did marry in 1874, it is said that the marriage reversed traditional gender roles. Eugène Manet, brother of famed Impressionist Édouard Manet, was an amateur painter, she the professional. He even posed for Morisot's portraits, which was unusual for the time.

AN UNFINISHED CANVAS

Morisot was a quintessential Impressionist, working in rapid, sketch-like brushstrokes without making preliminary sketches, often leaving canvases unfinished.

MOTHERHOOD IN ART

With art often providing an outlet for human experience, it's no surprise that maternal relationships and motherhood have been explored by many artists in multiple ways.

Paintings that celebrate motherhood

The Madonna of the Carnation - Leonardo da Vinci
Self-Portrait with her Daughter, Julie - Élisabeth Vigée Le Brun
Romance - Cecile Walton
Mother and Child - Gustav Klimt
The Child's Bath - Mary Cassatt
Radiant Baby - Keith Haring

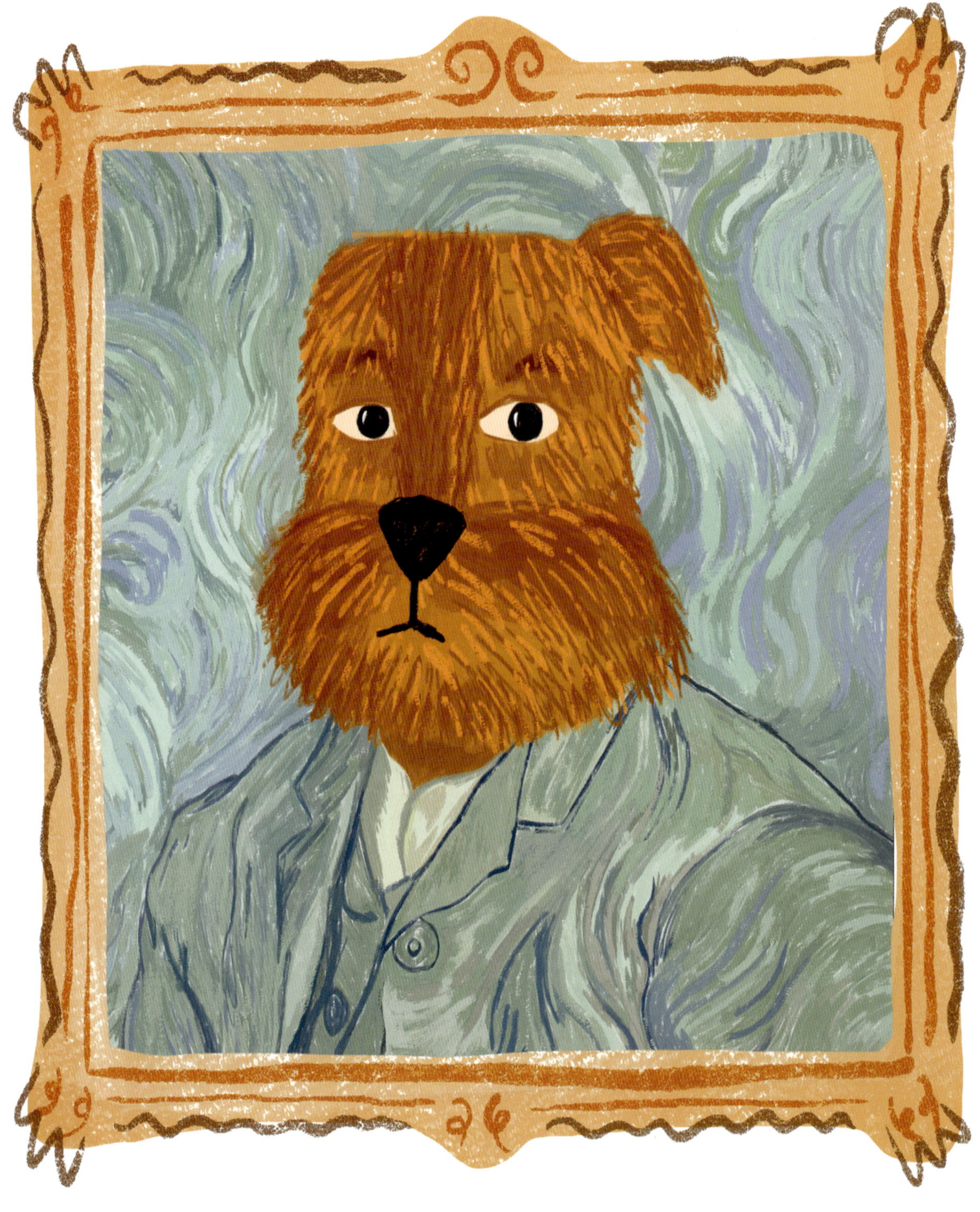

SELF—PORTRAIT 1889
BY VINCENT VAN GOGH

Working in the late 1800s, Vincent van Gogh developed an artistic style that pushed the boundaries of what was accepted as 'portraiture', creating paintings that were shockingly different from anything seen before. His self-portraits proved far from popular, however, and many critics accused van Gogh of barking up the wrong tree with his bold new approach.

In *Self-Portrait 1889*, the artist is faithfully depicted with red hair and beard, gaunt features and a hangdog expression. Composed of thick, heavy impasto strokes, there is a feeling of depth and movement to the background; like a dog frenziedly chasing its tail, the striking, restless brushstrokes appear to be in constant motion. The figure itself, in contrast, appears quite static, reflecting a rare sense of peace that the artist felt at the time of this painting, one of his final self-portraits.

A WINDOW TO THE SOUL

While artists throughout history have explored self-representation, van Gogh's dogged focus on self-portraits holds particular significance. These introspective works offer a window into his mind, allowing us to witness his artistic evolution and gain insights into his thoughts and emotions. Van Gogh's self-portraits provide a personal narrative, documenting his journey as an artist and a human being.

His radical reinvention of the genre as a way to express the inner life of the artist paved the way for other serial self-portraitists such as Frida Kahlo and Antony Gormley.

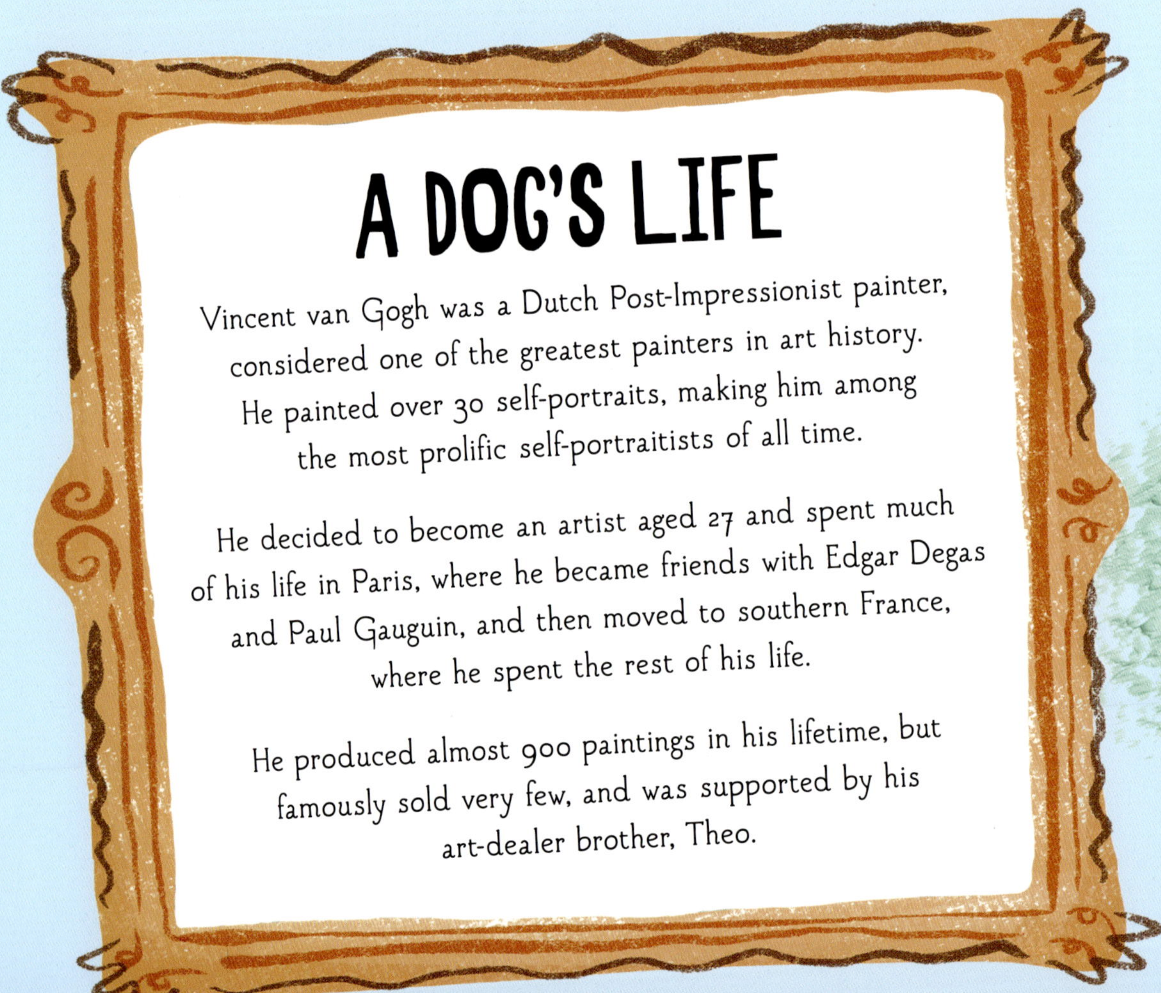

A DOG'S LIFE

Vincent van Gogh was a Dutch Post-Impressionist painter, considered one of the greatest painters in art history. He painted over 30 self-portraits, making him among the most prolific self-portraitists of all time.

He decided to become an artist aged 27 and spent much of his life in Paris, where he became friends with Edgar Degas and Paul Gauguin, and then moved to southern France, where he spent the rest of his life.

He produced almost 900 paintings in his lifetime, but famously sold very few, and was supported by his art-dealer brother, Theo.

PEN TO PAPER

Self-portraiture was a medium van Gogh used
to understand himself, but we can tell just as
much about this tortured artist from the letters
he exchanged with his brother. He had an
almost compulsive need to share his thoughts
and feelings, both on canvas and through
the written word.

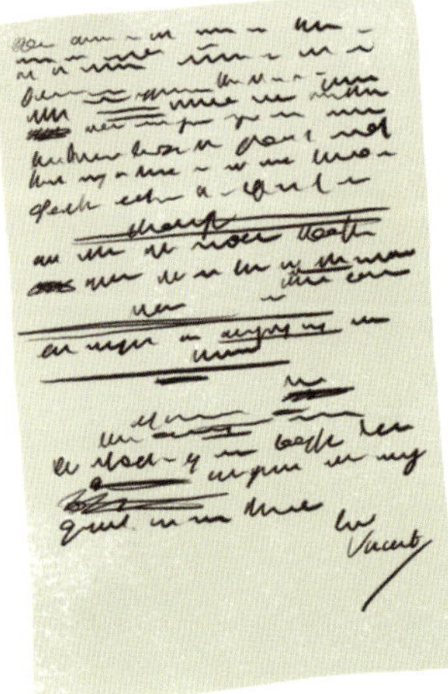

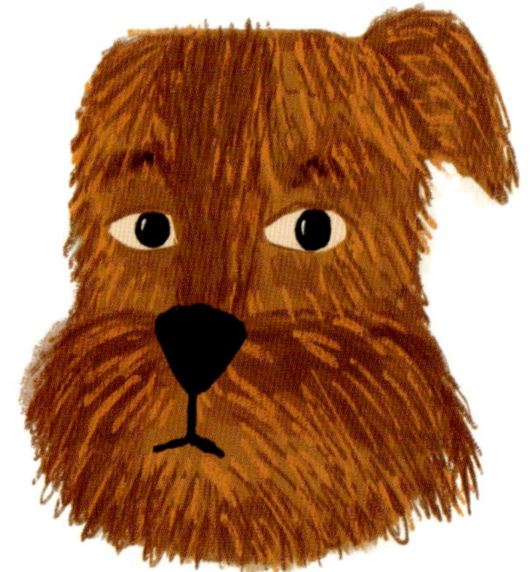

MIXED EMOTIONS

His 36 self-portraits depict a range of emotions,
from joy to despair. He explored themes such
as love, sorrow, loneliness, and death through
his art. These themes become more apparent
when viewed through the face
of a single subject.

EVOLUTION OF AN ARTIST

Van Gogh also used his self-portraits as a way
of developing and practising new techniques.
The evolution of the swirling impasto strokes
is most clear when comparing the dark,
earthy hues of his early work with his more
recognizable later paintings.

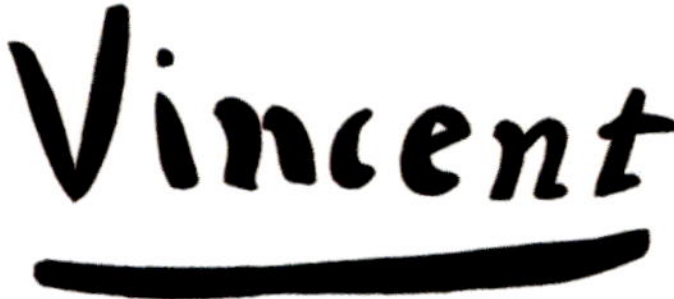

A SIGN OF THE TIMES

Van Gogh signed his paintings simply
'Vincent' – this is possibly because in
France, where he was living, people
struggled to pronounce 'van Gogh'.

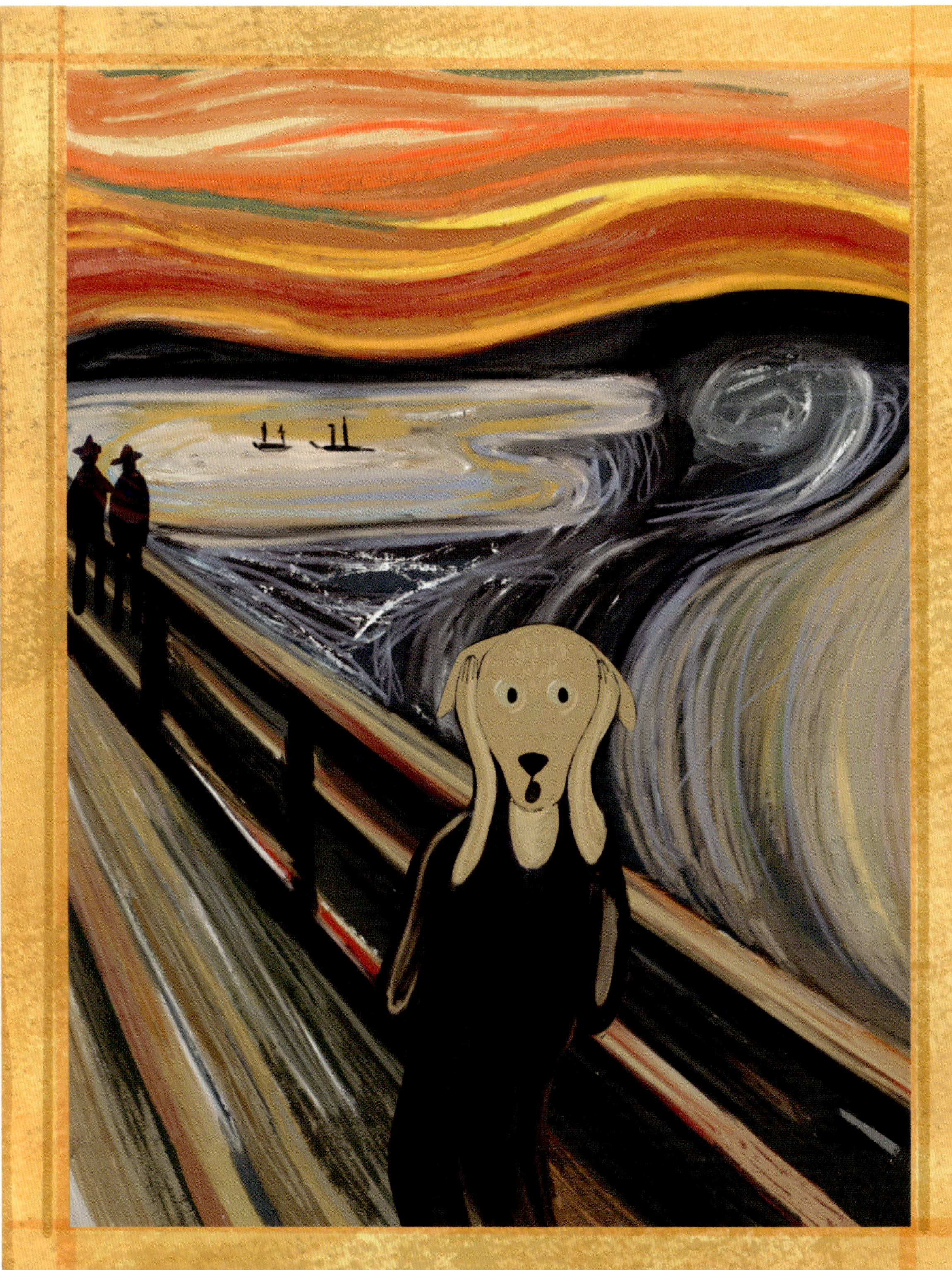

THE SCREAM BY EDVARD MUNCH

With vigorous brushstrokes and a fiery palette that belies its deeply soulful side, *The Scream* is a portrait with a bark that's worse than its bite. Painted by Edvard Munch in 1893, it captures a moment of primal, unadulterated anxiety. The painting's intense, swirling brushstrokes and distorted forms convey a sense of deep inner turmoil, reflecting the angst of modern life.

Munch's use of bold, exaggerated lines and his emphasis on expression over realism were revolutionary for the time and played a key role in the development of the Expressionist art movement. The subject's agonized face has become an instantly recognizable symbol of human despair.

Beyond its artistic innovations, *The Scream* is important for its exploration of universal human emotions such as fear, loneliness and grief. Munch's work perfectly and dramatically captures the intense emotional experiences that are part of the human condition, making it a triumph of art but also of emotional expression. Its popularity further emphasizes its enduring significance in both art history and contemporary culture.

EXPRESS YOURSELF

The essense of Expressionism in portraiture is an emphasis
not on photorealistic portrayals of external scenes, but rather
on conveying the mood and mental condition of the artist
or subject at the time of the painting. Using bold pigments,
distorted angles and flattened forms helped artists to
reflect the darker side of life.

A movement that flourished in Western Europe in the early
part of the twentieth century, other prominent Expressionists
include Wassily Kandinsky, Emil Nolde and Egon Schiele.

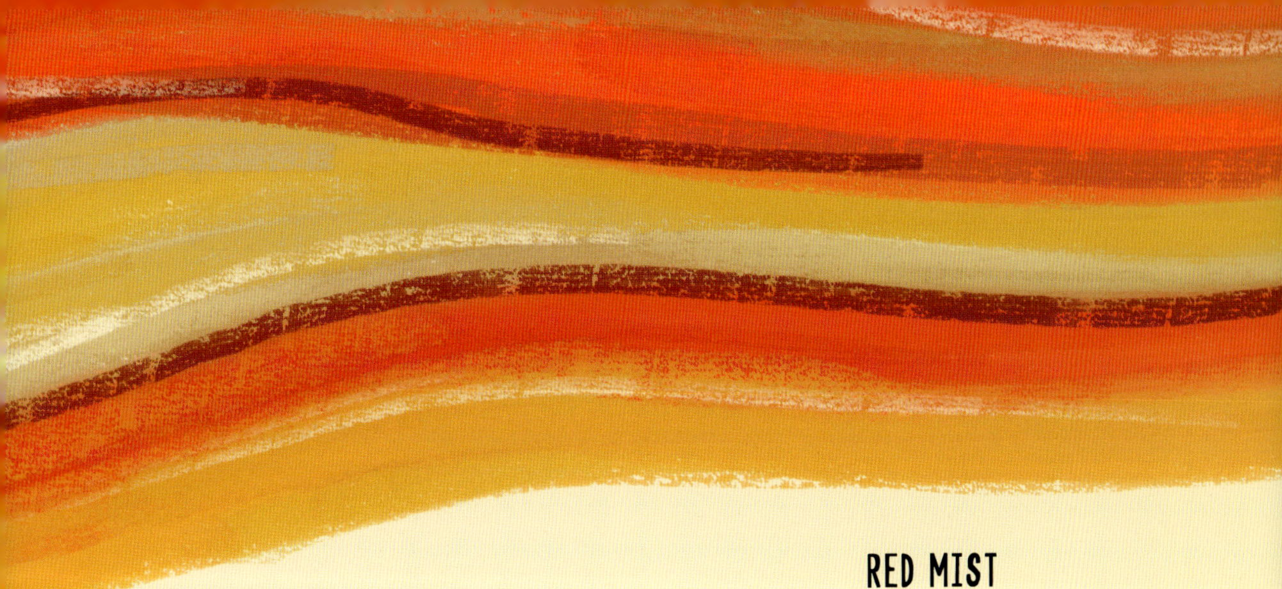

> **"It is not the chair which is to be painted but what the human being has felt in relation to it."**
> **Edvard Munch**

RED MIST

Possibly inspired by a volcanic sunset seen by Munch in 1883, the aggressively red-orange sky seems to perfectly capture a 'scream of nature'.

BOBBING BOATS

The two boats, bobbing peacefully in the background, provide a contrast to the gut-wrenching horror experienced by the subject and perhaps serve as a reminder of calmer, less angst-ridden times.

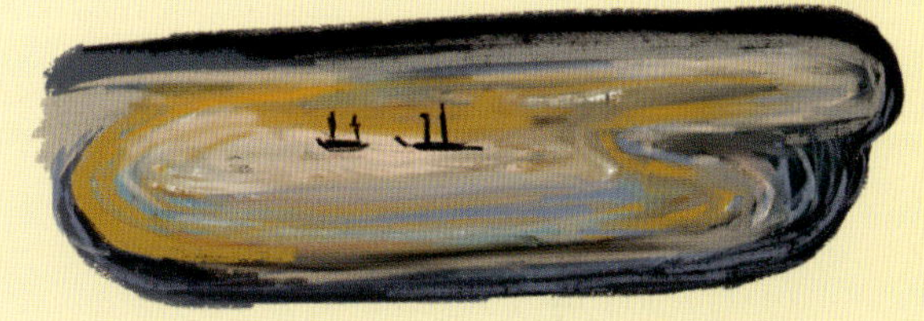

POWERFUL MESSAGE

An inscription scrawled on the painting – can only have been painted by a madman – baffled experts for years. However, art historians now believe Munch himself scrawled the line in response to the critical reception the work received when it was first exhibited. Munch was hurt by critics' speculation regarding his mental health, as he had a family history of mental illness.

"Kan Kun være malet af en gal Mand!

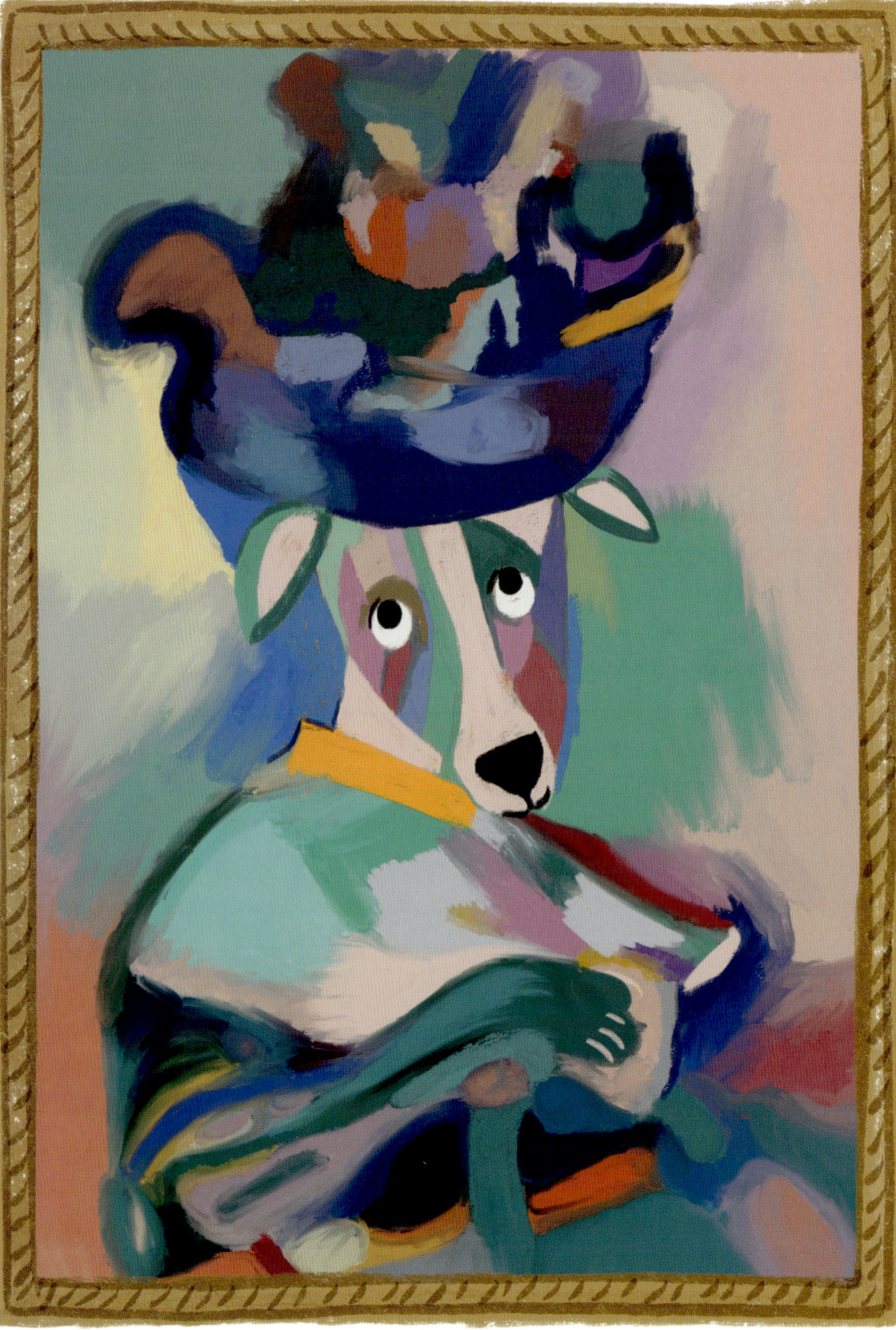

WOMAN WITH A HAT BY HENRI MATISSE

Unveiled in 1905, Henri Matisse's boldly rendered portrait of his wife, Amélie, lit the touchpaper of a modern art explosion that was to revolutionize twentieth-century art.

A landmark portrait, Matisse's *Woman with a Hat* marked a departure from the portraiture of the past with his use of bold, non-naturalistic shades and expressive brushwork. His audacious approach to palette and form sparked outrage among critics when the painting was first shown at the *Salon d'Automne* in Paris, but thrilled fellow avant-garde artists, who began to challenge traditional techniques and explore new artistic possibilities for themselves.

One of the key works of the Fauvist movement, *Woman with a Hat* has become an iconic painting, symbolizing the daringly expressive nature of early modern art. It represents a shift towards abstraction and an opportunity for artists to run freely off-leash, contributing significantly to the evolution of art styles today.

THE 'WILD BEASTS'

Exploding onto the canvas in a riot of bright hues, vigorously applied, Fauvism first emerged at the beginning of the twentieth century as a reaction to the more muted palettes of the Impressionists.

An interest in new scientific theory led to artists such as Matisse, André Derain and Paul Braque experimenting with placing complementary tones next to each other to increase their visual impact.

Fauvism is often compared to Expressionism, as the two movements share the same use of bold shades and spontaneous brushwork that led artists to be known as the 'Fauves', or 'wild beasts'.

Many Fauvist artists went on to pioneer new art styles including Cubism, while Matisse continued his Fauvist use of pigment, shape and bold brushstrokes throughout his career.

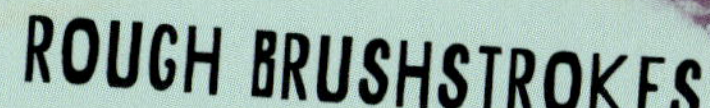

ROUGH BRUSHSTROKES

Typical of Fauvist works are the rough, fluid brushstrokes. Many people who saw the work believed it to be incomplete, such was the nature of the finish.

WHEEL OF FORTUNE

In this painting, brisk strokes of paint – blues, greens and reds – form an energetic, expressive view of the woman. Fauvists liked to pair complementary shades, chosen from opposite sides of the wheel, for maximum impact.

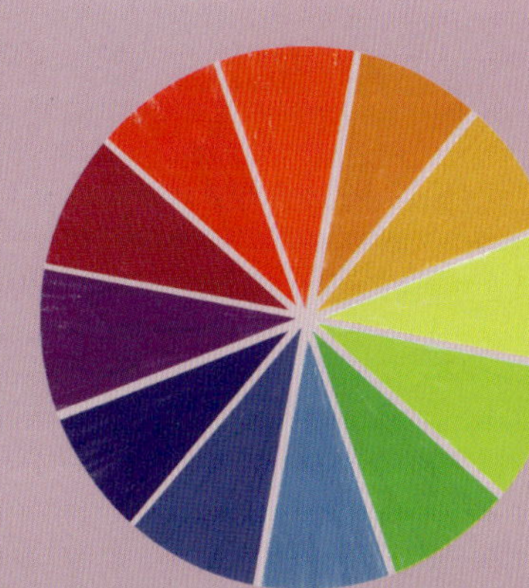

FANCY ACCESSORIES

Amélie is portrayed in a typical bourgeois outfit of the early twentieth century, with an elaborate hat, gloves and a fan.

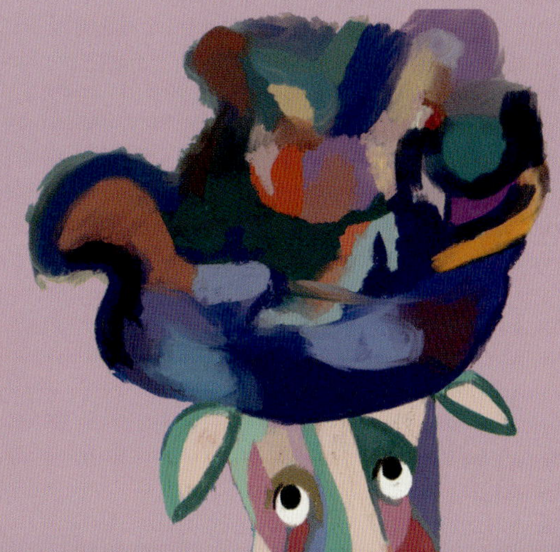

BLACK IS BACK

When Matisse was asked to describe the true appearance of his wife's dress he replied 'Black, of course!'.

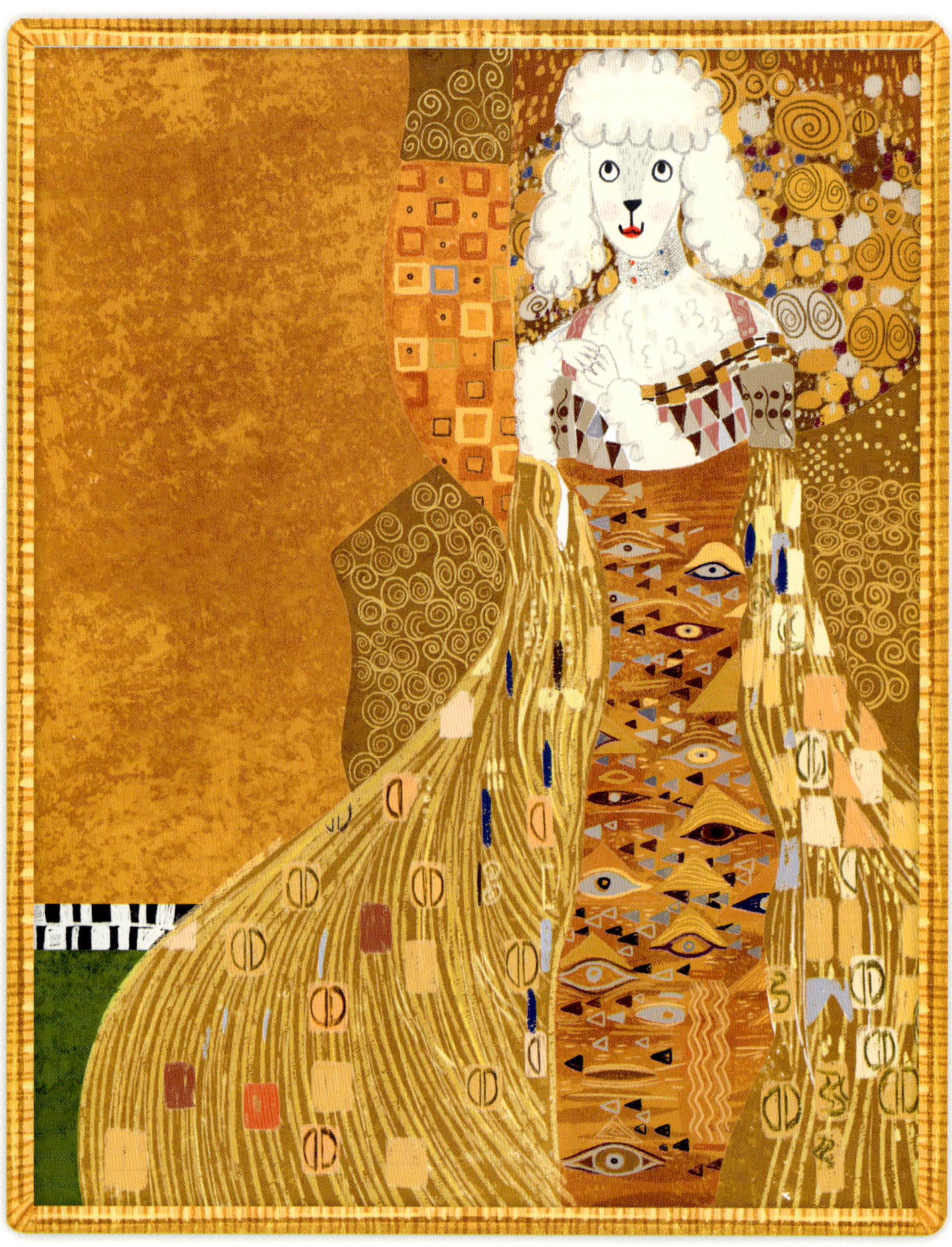

PORTRAIT OF ADELE BLOCH-BAUER I BY GUSTAV KLIMT

Klimt's 1907 masterpiece in shimmering gold is the final and most representative work of Klimt's 'golden phase'. This portrait became a key work of the Art Nouveau period and one of Klimt's most famous paintings.

An Austrian symbolist painter and one of the most prominent members of the Vienna Secession movement, Klimt was commissioned in 1903 by wealthy industrialist Ferdinand Bloch-Bauer to paint a portrait of his wife, Adele. Adele Bloch-Bauer was herself a significant figure on the Vienna art scene, hosting a famous art salon and using her wealth and status to support artists like Klimt. The resulting portrait, which shows Bloch-Bauer resplendent on a throne-like chair of shimmering gold, took almost four years to complete.

Gustav Klimt's *Portrait of Adele Bloch-Bauer I* is one of the most recognizable portraits in art history today. It epitomizes the opulent, ornamental style of the Vienna Secession movement. It also serves to highlight the importance of women like Adele Bloch-Bauer in helping artists like Klimt.

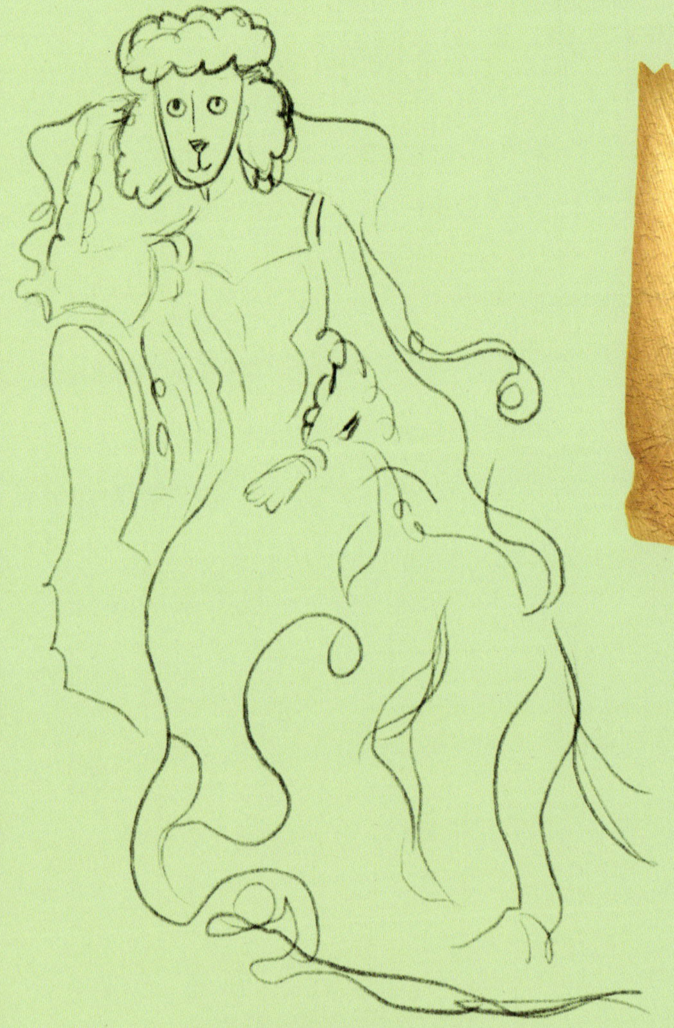

GOLD LEAF

The Austrian artist had seen his father work as a goldsmith, and the material held deep personal significance to him. In his 'golden phase', he used gold leaf and oil paint, combining the two materials to create the dazzling effect that has become synonymous with his work.

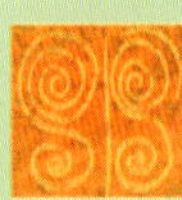
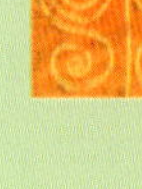
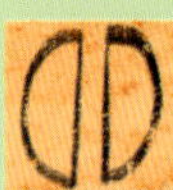

MOSAIC EFFECT

Klimt studied the Byzantine gold mosaics in the Basilica of San Vitale in Ravenna, Italy, which had a huge influence on his 'golden phase'. The golden square and circular decorative parts covering the dress and backrest of the armchair seem to have been inspired by the Basilica.

GET PREPPED

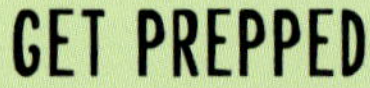

Klimt dedicated years to perfecting the portrait, creating hundreds of sketches in the process. Adele Bloch-Bauer and her husband were important figures on the art scene at the time, so Klimt was under pressure to get the painting absolutely right.

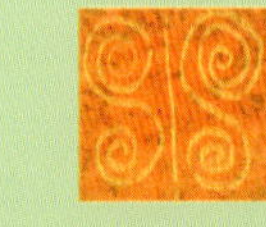

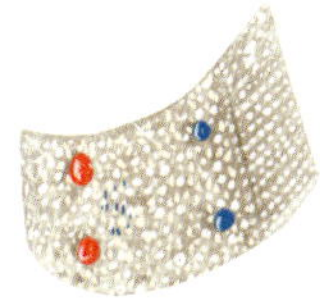

DIAMONDS ARE A DOG'S BEST FRIEND

The air of shimmering opulence is reinforced by the inclusion of a sparkling diamond necklace, a present from Bloch-Bauer's husband.

ALL-SEEING EYE

The Egyptian-style motifs on the dress were perhaps included for amuletic purposes, as Bloch-Bauer experienced health problems throughout her life.

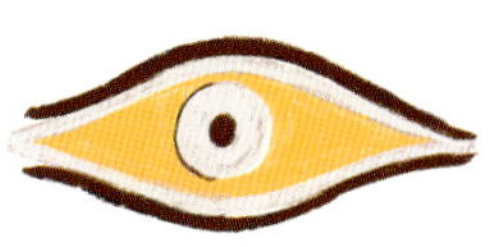

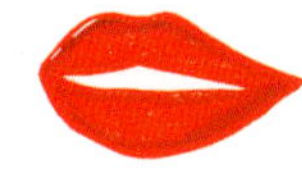

NATURAL FACE

Only the face is shown realistically, a trademark of Klimt's portraiture, which gives the ethereal impression of the subject floating above a shining sea of dazzling gold.

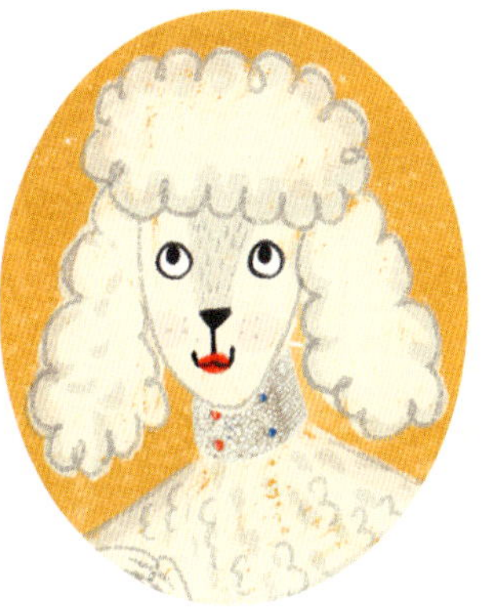

PUCKER UP

Along with her flushed cheeks, the red lips convey attraction, Could this hint at some truth to the rumours of a love interest between the artist and sitter?

FLOWING GOWN

The elaborate gown is typical of the Art Nouveau period. Klimt was not always so avant garde in his style, however. Early in his career he was awarded the Emperor's Prize for his work painting the old Burgtheater, paving the way for his career as a classical portraitist. However, rather than running with this traditional style, Klimt turned towards the radical new styles of the Art Nouveau.

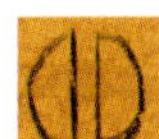

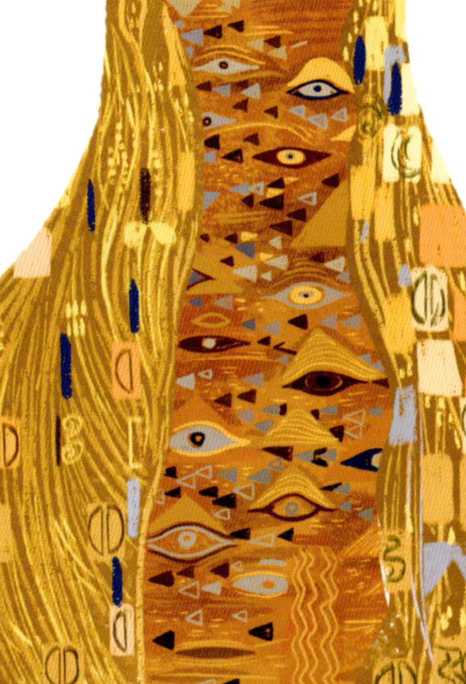

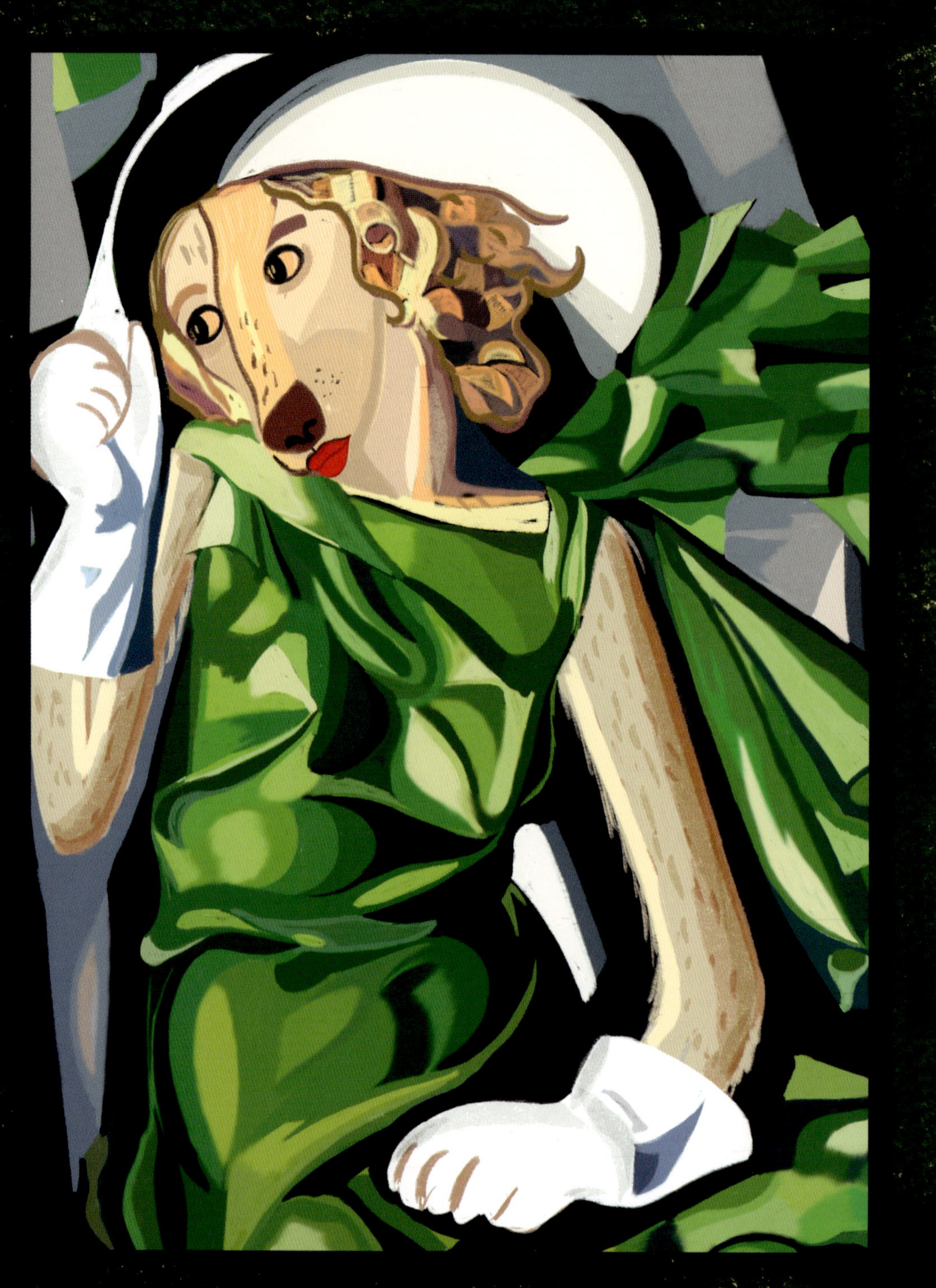

YOUNG LADY WITH GLOVES BY TAMARA DE LEMPICKA

Tamara de Lempicka's *Young Lady with Gloves*, painted in 1930, is a quintessential example of the Art Deco movement and one of the most iconic portraits of the twentieth century. Capturing the essence of modern femininity during the interwar period, this painting reflects a contemporary fascination with elegance, sophistication, and the allure of the independent woman.

The subject, a fashionable, sophisticated woman captured in a confident pose, epitomizes the strong, liberated woman of the 1920s and 1930s. Lempicka's sculptural style, characterized by precise, clean lines and geometric shapes, perfectly reflects the Art Deco aesthetic, blending classical influences with modern sensibilities.

Young Lady with Gloves, with its glamorous yet empowered portrayal of womenhood, challenges traditional notions of femininity and captures the exuberance of the Bright Young Things of the Roaring Twenties. The work has had a lasting influence on both the portrayal of women in art and the broader cultural perception of female empowerment.

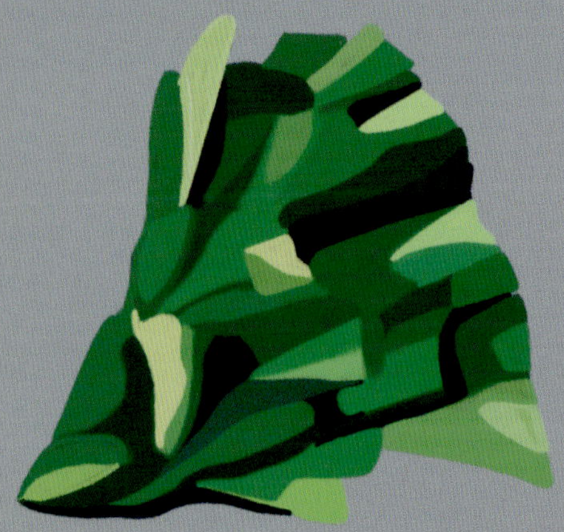

DON'T BE A SQUARE

Lempicka was a proponent of 'synthetic cubism'. This meant that she sought to flatten images so there was no sense of three-dimensional space. To achieve this effect, Lempicka built up images out of small geometric shapes in varying shades.

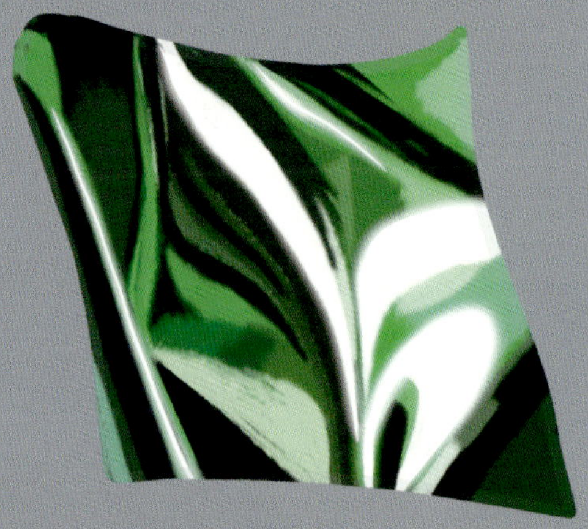

PAINT PALETTE

Metallic oil paints lend a glamorous sheen to the dress. The reflection of light helps bring both a sense of movement to the dress and a voluptuous, attractive quality to the figure.

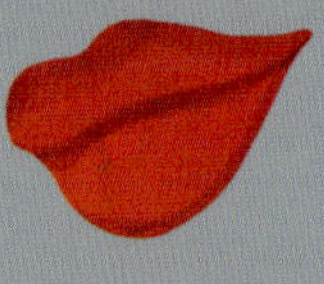

LIPS

Bright red lips were a calling card of Lempicka's portraits, which depicted strong, confident women, unafraid to express themselves.

PAW IN GLOVE

The subject's opulent outfit, from her elegant gloves to her fashionable hat, makes her appear stylish and refined, showing the growing interest in personal style and expression of the period and reflecting contemporary fashion trends.

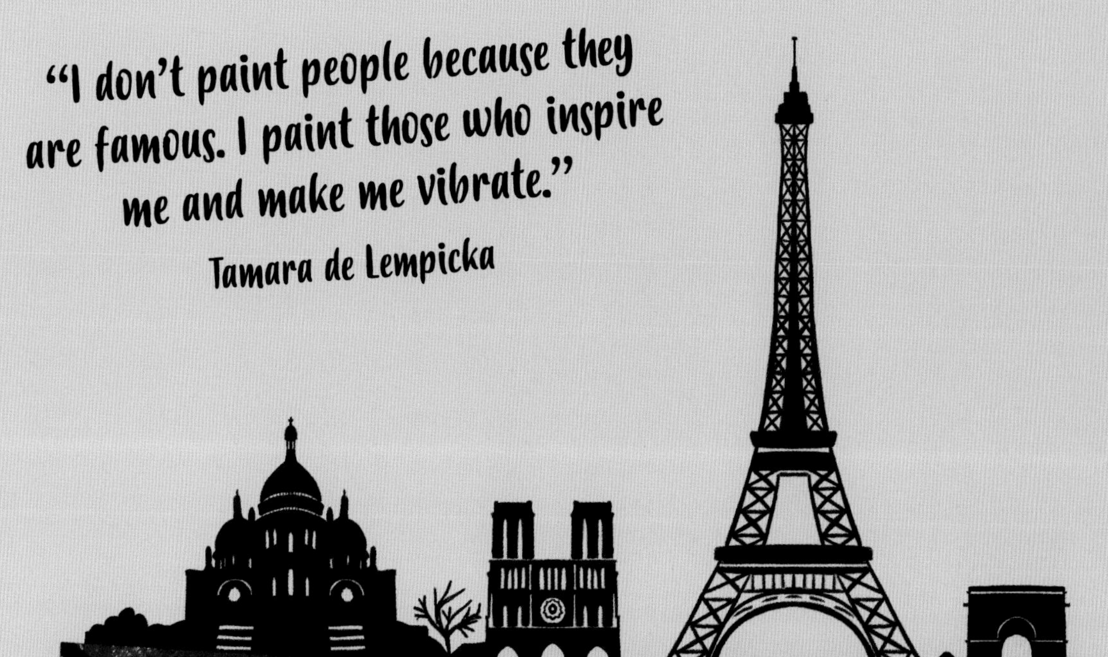

PORTRAIT OF THE ARTIST

Born in 1898 to a wealthy family, Lempicka lived the quintessential bohemian life, first in Paris and later in America, and was a popular portrait painter with the 'It' crowd of the time. A glamorous figure on the Parisian art scene, she is best-known for her theatrical portraits of fashionable subjects.

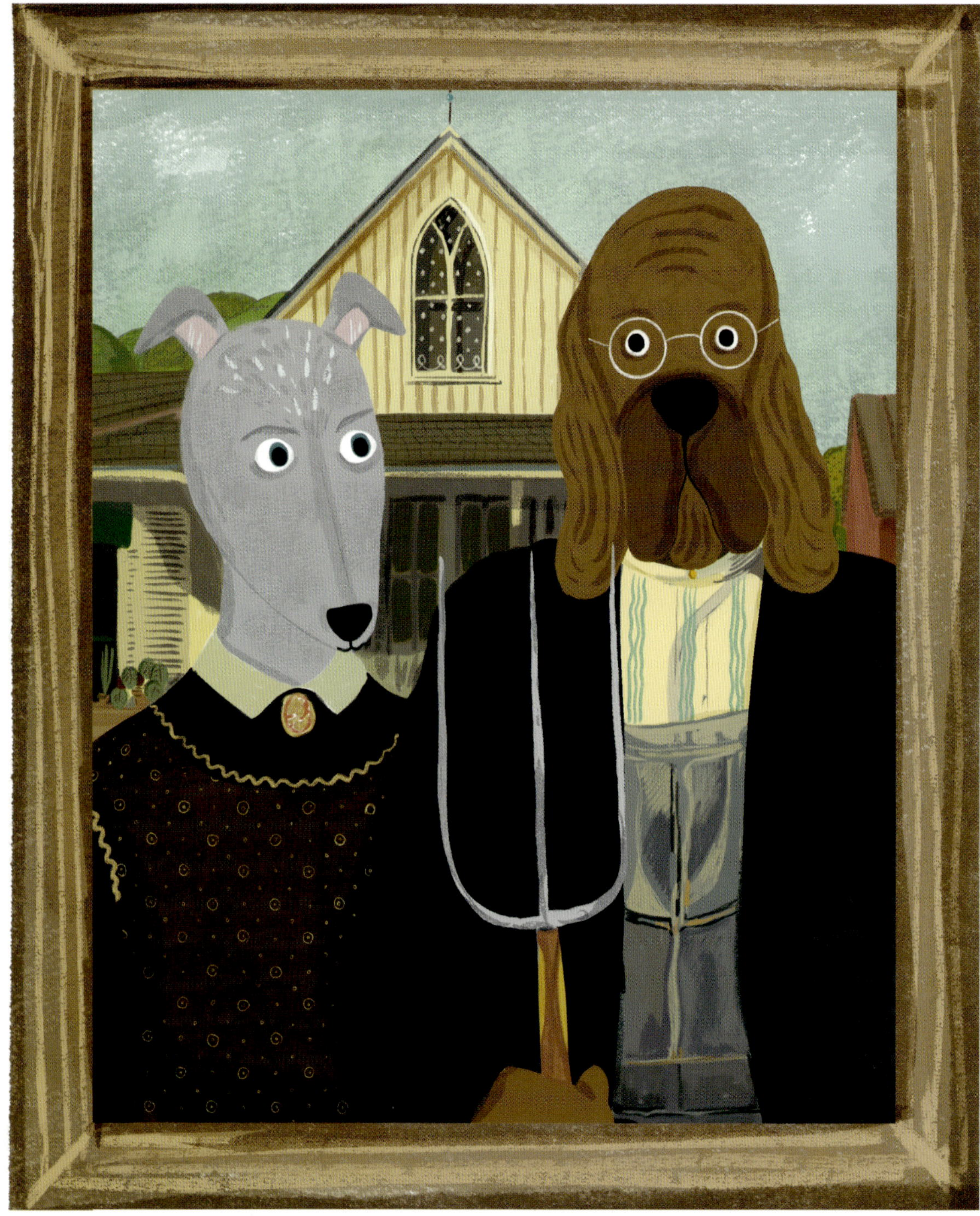

AMERICAN GOTHIC
BY GRANT WOOD

Offered by artist Grant Wood as a nostalgic vision of traditional Americana (or, as some interpreted, a satirical comment about 'small town' Midwesterners being out of step with the modern world) at the beginning of America's Great Depression, *American Gothic* was an instant hit when it was first exhibited in 1930.

Posed in a way that resembles long-exposure photographs of families from the early part of the twentieth century, this portrait was carefully orchestrated and painted in separate parts. Wood had his sister Nan and his dentist, Dr McKeeby, pose separately for the painting, but they are not posing as themselves, rather playing the parts of a generic couple of the past, thought to be father and daughter. Their poses and facial expressions are ambiguous – the man stern, the woman resigned or sad. Both figures are imbued with symbolic elements – from their dress to the pitchfork to the building itself.

Whatever Wood's intended meaning, today, *American Gothic* is one of the most enduring emblems of Americana and has sparked countless parodies, proving that even serious art can have a playful side.

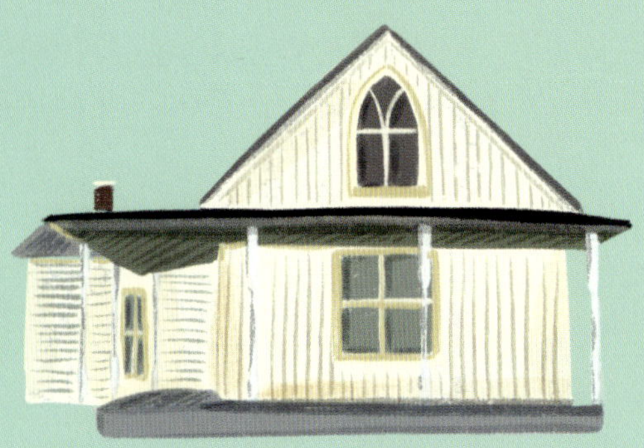

GOTHIC HOUSE

The very title of the painting is a reference to the architecture of a house that Wood happened across, and inspired him to imagine the lives of the people who might live there.

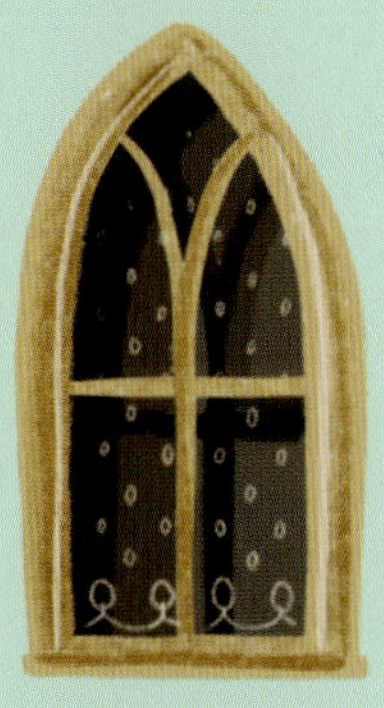

WINDOW DRESSING

Closed, darkened windows were a mourning custom in Victorian America, which, along with the expression on the woman's face, gives weight to the idea that she may be grieving something or someone.

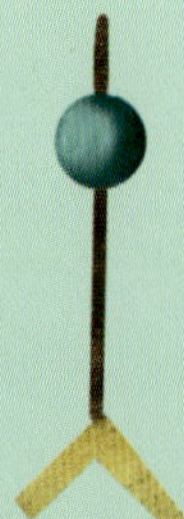

WHATEVER THE WEATHER

It has been suggested that the globe at the top of the weather vane represents the planet, Pluto, which was discovered in 1930, the year Wood painted the portrait.

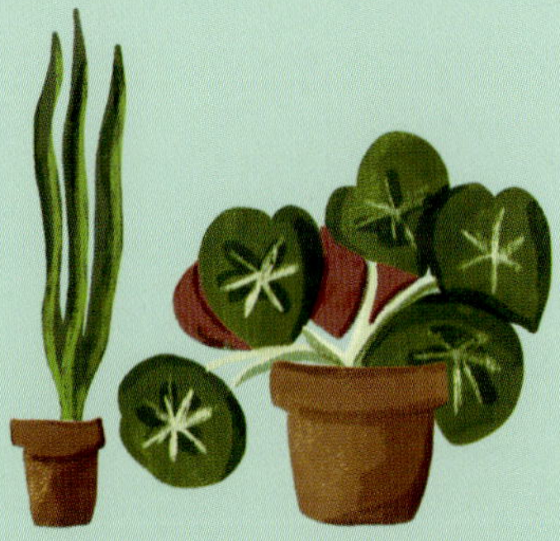

DEEP-ROOTED PLANTS

The plants on the porch of the house are common motifs in Wood's work – the mother-in-law's tongue and beefsteak begonia, also appear in Wood's 1929 portrait of his mother, *Woman with Plants*.

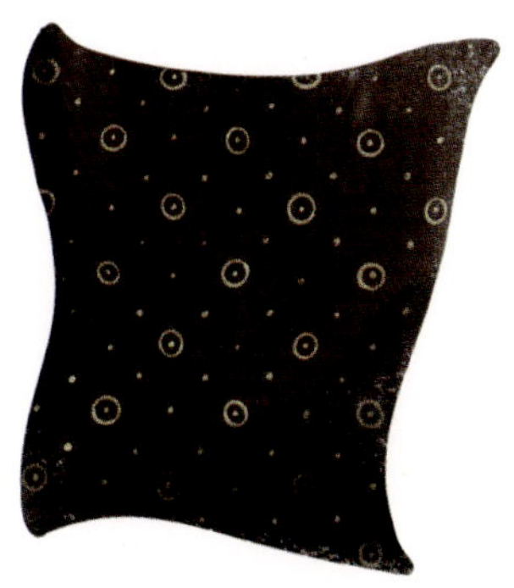

SUNDAY BEST

The couple's clothing indicates they have made
an effort to dress up, perhaps inviting the viewer
to speculate on what seems to be an important
moment in their lives.

> **"It is the depth and intensity of
> an artist's experience that are
> the first importance in art."**
> Grant Wood

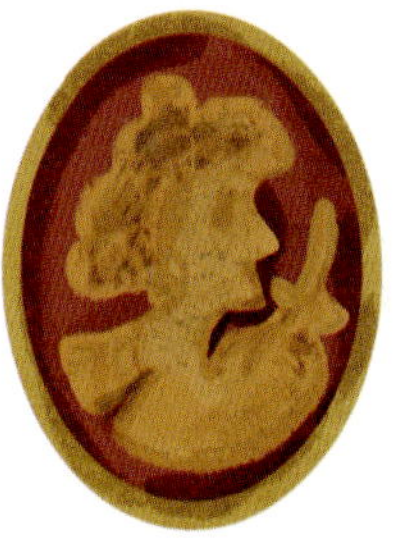

NO ENTRY

The pitchfork is often referred to as
the 'third character' in the painting. Its shape is echoed
on the man's overalls, on his face and on the upper
window of the house, and acts as a powerful 'no entry'
symbol. Some have interpreted the pitchfork-wielding
farmer as the guardian of the gates of hell, Hades,
and points to the woman's cameo brooch, containing
a classical representation of the kidnapped goddess,
Persephone, to back up the theory.

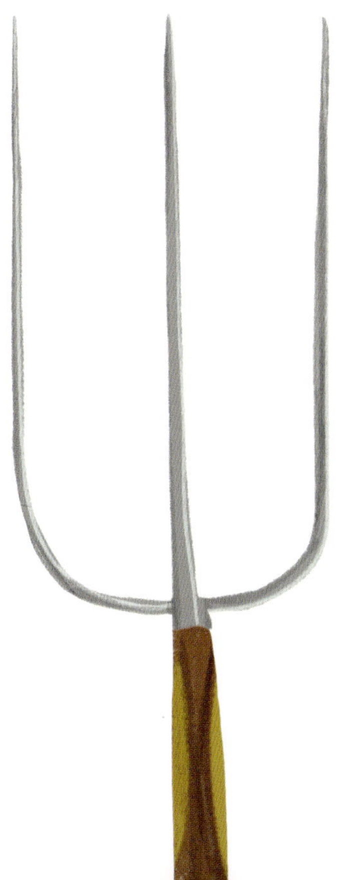

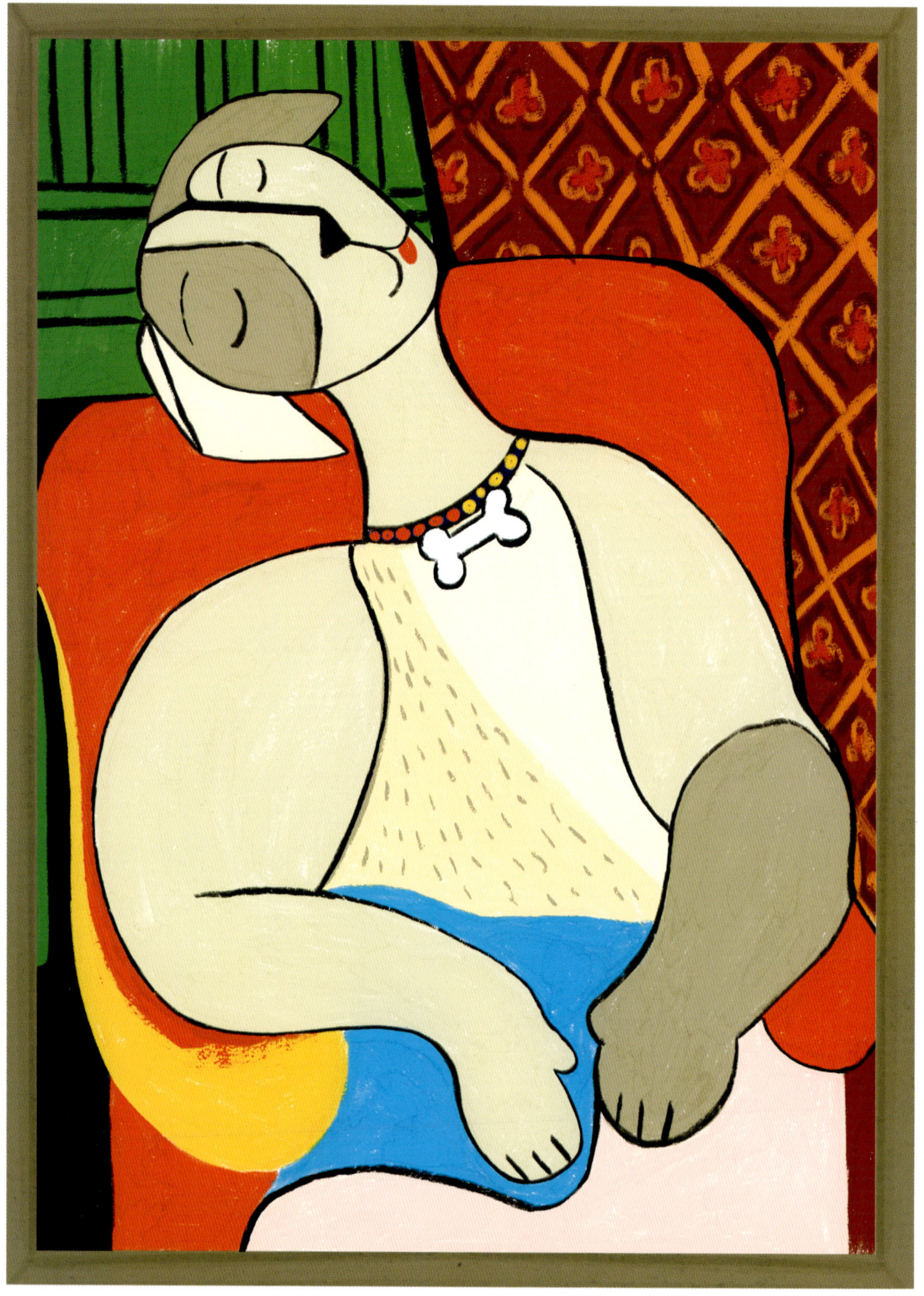

THE DREAM
BY PABLO PICASSO

The Dream, or *Le Rêve*, is a 1932 work by Pablo Picasso, depicting his mistress, Marie-Thérèse Walter, in a relaxed, dreamlike state. The bold use of pigment and fluid, organic shapes are in contrast to the striking, angular lines of some of the artist's other best-known works. Despite this, *The Dream* is one of Picasso's most recognizable pieces, and notable as one of the most expensive paintings ever sold.

While many regard it as a Cubist work, it could also be categorized as a work of Picasso's Surrealist period, while the high-contrast palette points to Fauvist influences. The genius of the work lies in the way Picasso has deconstructed the face and figure in the Cubist style, while keeping the pose, mood and character of the subject recognizable.

Perhaps the most influential artist of the twentieth century, Picasso was constantly challenging classification, as his unique ideas produced work in styles never seen before. *The Dream* showcases his mastery of form and symbolism, blurring the boundaries between reality and imagination. The portrait expresses the artist's relationship with the subject, showcasing the complexity of human emotions with its gentle, dreamlike composition.

NOSE AND MOUTH

The 'split' face symbolizes duality and Picasso's desire
to show fantasy and reality alongside each other. He was
interested in the idea, central to Surrealism, that reality
is shaped by dreams and that the two can be
impossible to separate.

CLOSED EYES

The subject's eyes are closed in a peaceful
pose, conveying vulnerability and
an innocent, dreamlike state.

CUBIST FACE

Picasso also used the Cubist 'split'
effect to show different perspectives
at the same time.

STARK CONTRASTS

The bright red and yellow of the armchair are echoed by
the red and yellow of the beads on the woman's necklace
and the red of her lips. The more muted secondary shades
in the background create contrast with the foreground, and
help lend the painting an air of passion.

> "Art is not the application of a canon of beauty
> but what the instinct and the brain can conceive
> beyond any canon. When we love a woman
> we don't start measuring her limbs."
>
> Pablo Picasso

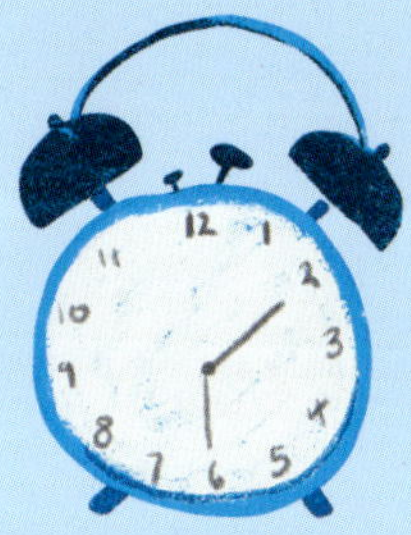

ON THE CLOCK

The Dream was finished by Picasso
in less than a day. He was painting
prolifically at the time as he wanted his
1932 retrospective to 'beat' one that his
artistic rival, Henri Matisse, had held
the previous year.

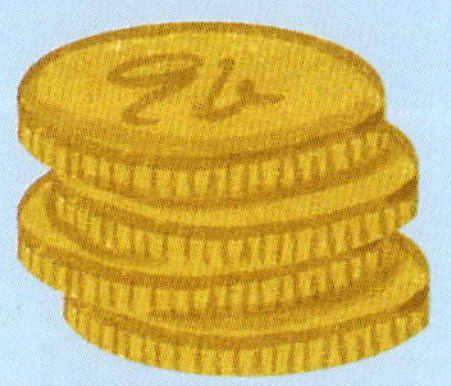

MONEY MATTERS

The Dream is one of the most expensive
paintings of all time. Marie-Thérèse has
been nicknamed Picasso's 'golden muse',
as paintings featuring her have typically
sold for particularly high prices.

Paintings by Picasso featuring the same muse

Girl Before a Mirror
The Dreamer
Nude in a Black Armchair
Two Girls Reading

LINE UP

Picasso played with shape and form with
oversimplified outlines that are fluid and
appear loose. The gentle curves of the figure
seem exaggerated because of the contrast
between these flowing lines and the geometric
patterns Picasso painted in the background.

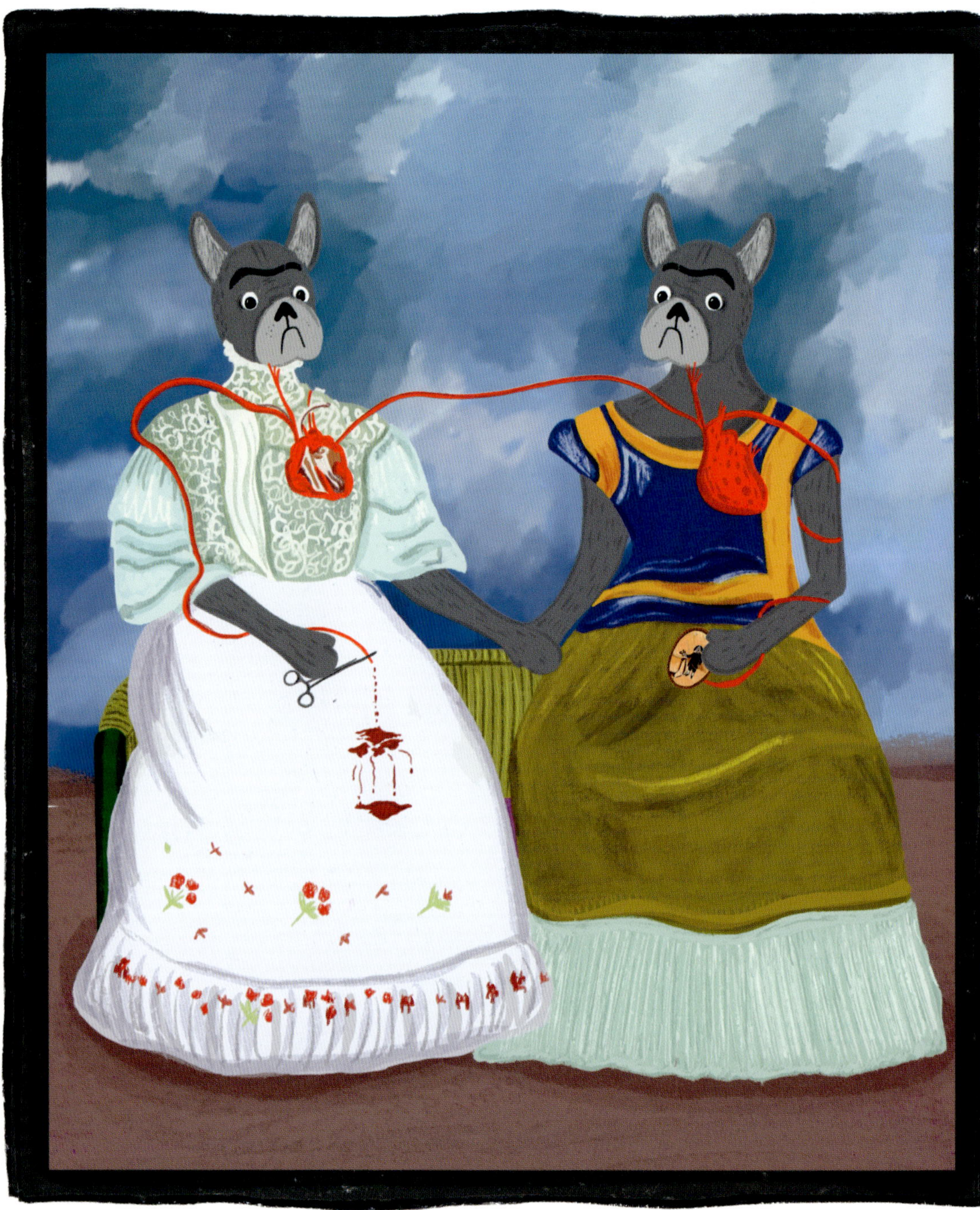

THE TWO FRIDAS BY FRIDA KAHLO

This double self-portrait, produced as Kahlo was going through her divorce from fellow artist Diego Rivera, reflects the heartbreak she felt during this tumultuous period. The appearance of the two figures has been said to represent the artist's two distinct 'personalities'. The European Frida is a version of the artist before she met Rivera. The figure in the traditional dress that she subsequently adopted is thought to represent the version that Rivera loved, while the European version, with wounded heart, the Frida he rejected.

As well as representing the artist's personal pain, the dual portrait reflects the universal struggle between inner self and outer persona, as well as a representation of Mexico's struggle with identity, torn between its indigenous roots and European colonialism. Kahlo was a strong advocate for Mexican culture and heritage, and her work played an important role in shaping the cultural and political landscape of her time.

In terms of technique, this unique and eye-catching painting exemplifies Kahlo's distinctive style, using bold hues and a flatness of plane that is characteristic of Mexican folk art.

PERSONAL VS POLITICAL

The Two Fridas is testament to Kahlo's skill in capturing complex emotions and ideologies. She cleverly links the universal struggle for identity and the human experience of pain and resilience to the contemporary political situation, making this an important and impactful work on all levels.

> "I paint self-portraits because I am so often alone, because I am the person I know best."
>
> Frida Kahlo

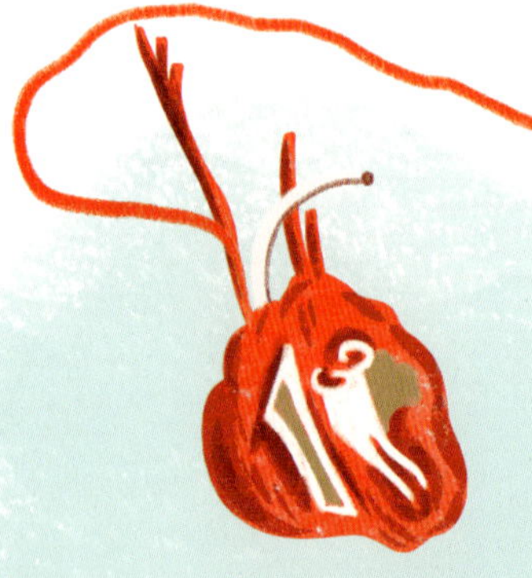

BLEEDING HEART

The heart of the Mexican Frida is whole and healthy, whereas the heart of the European Frida is wounded. Although the two figures appear independent of each other, a vein connecting the two may symbolize that despite their differences, the two are ultimately both inseparable parts of the same person.

ROLLING CLOUDS

The stormy sky looks ominous, reflecting Kahlo's inner turmoil, but the facial expressions of the two Fridas are strong and composed, demonstrating her resilience in the face of adversity.

FORCEPS

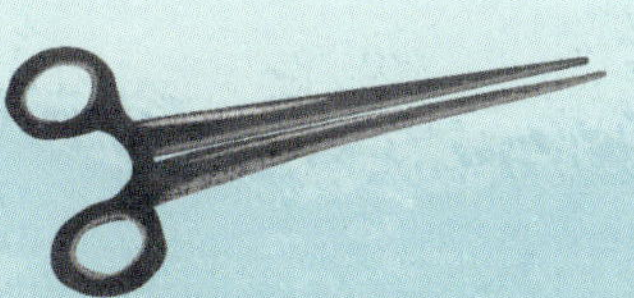

The European Frida holds a pair of hemostat forceps in an attempt to staunch a seemingly unstoppable flow of blood, perhaps as a sign that the artist's heartbreak is unrelenting.

LIFE IN MINIATURE

The Mexican Frida clutches a miniature portrait of Rivera – two of the most important artists of the twentieth century, Kahlo and Rivera painted each other throughout the course of their tempestuous 25-year relationship.

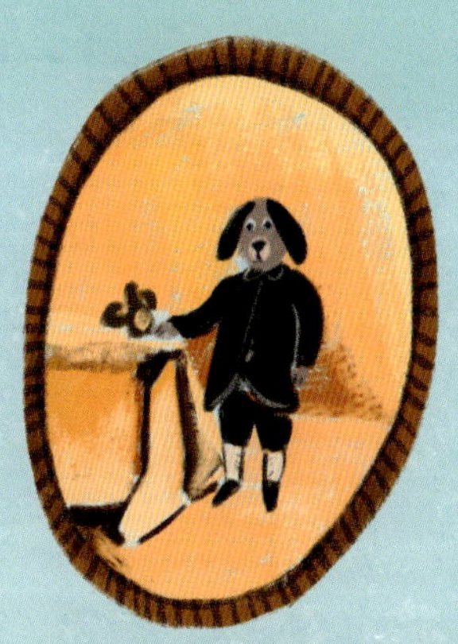

FLOWER EMBROIDERY

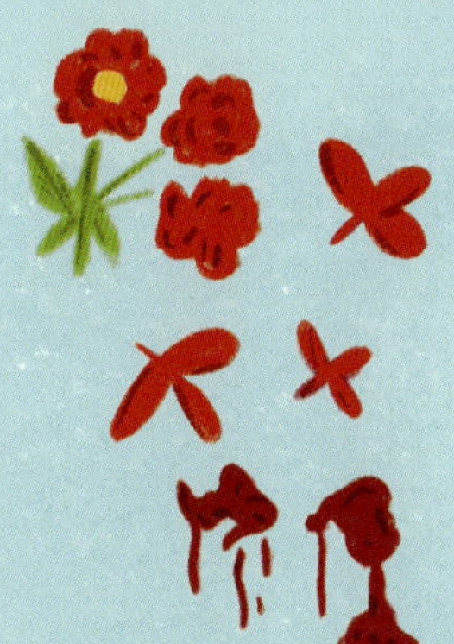

In the portrait, the small embroidered flowers of Kahlo's European-style dress blend with the dripping splotches of blood, perhaps as a sign that Frida felt it was this part of herself that had been rejected by her husband.

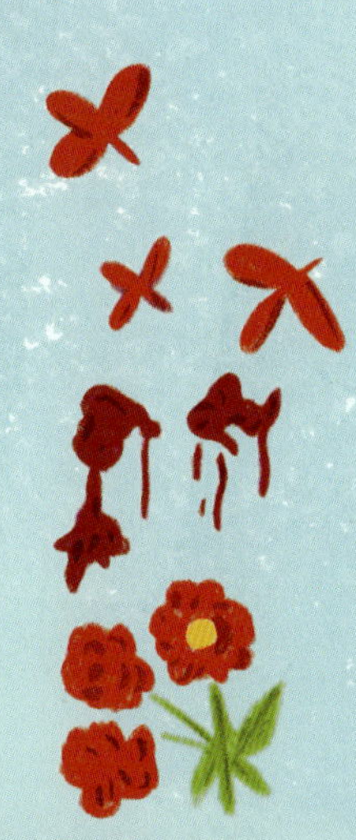

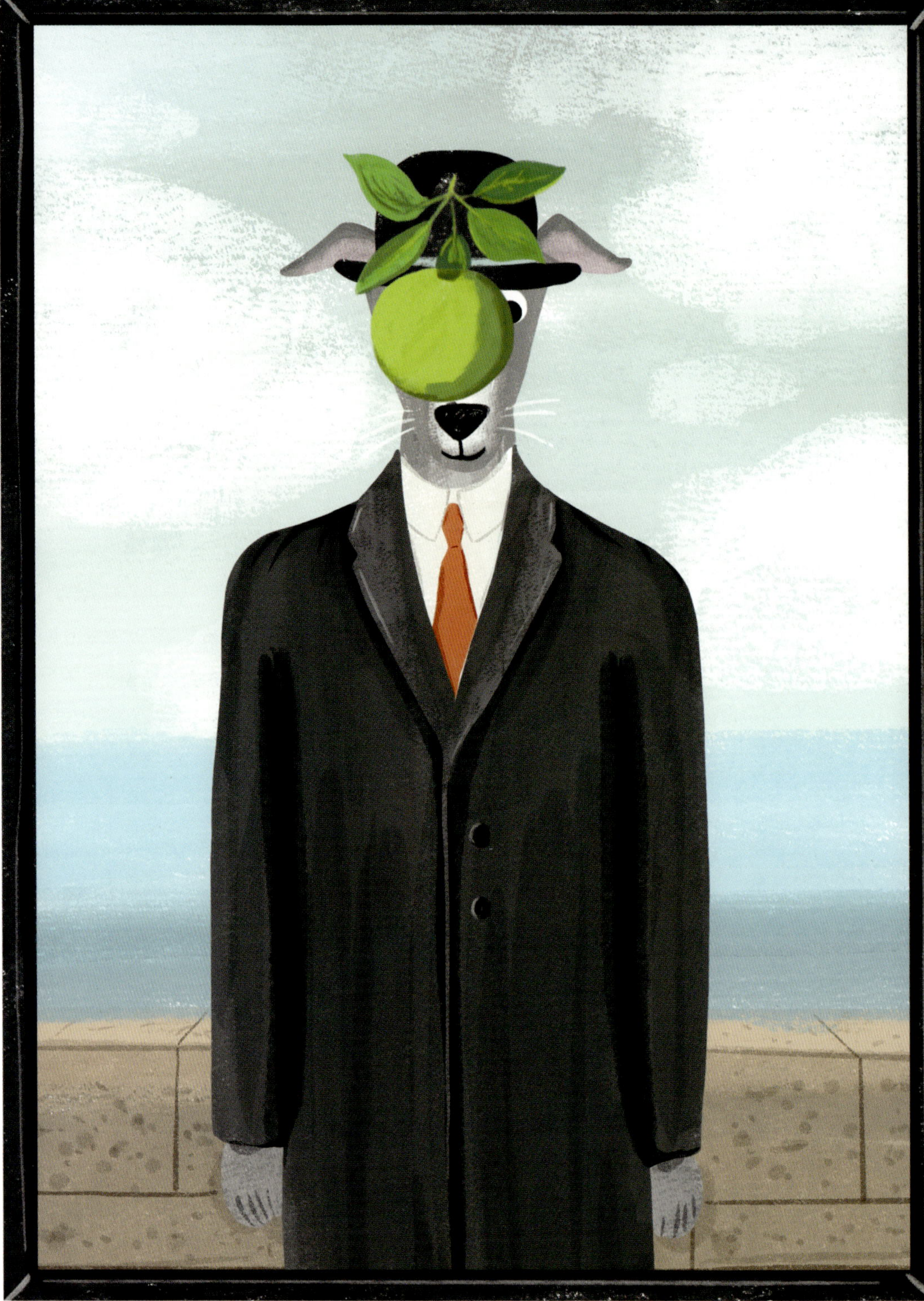

THE SON OF MAN
BY RENE MAGRITTE

A prominent figure of the Surrealist movement, Magritte's quirkily mysterious 1964 work, *The Son of Man*, cemented his place in the portrait artists' hall of fame and remains a significant and influential piece in the Surrealist canon.

Featuring a smartly dressed man in a bowler hat, his face partly obscured by a floating apple, the portrait seamlessly blends elements of the everyday with the bizarre, prompting viewers to reflect on the tension between appearance and reality, as well as the line between the conscious and the subconscious. With meticulous attention to detail, Magritte's precise rendering of ordinary elements in dreamlike contexts has fascinated art lovers since it was first shown. The subject of many and varied interpretations, it is generally agreed that the painting evokes Magritte's favourite themes of hidden identity, mystery and the subconscious mind.

The Son of Man has become an iconic image in popular culture. The combination of striking composition and enigmatic symbolism make for an unforgettable portrait that has sparked imaginations for decades.

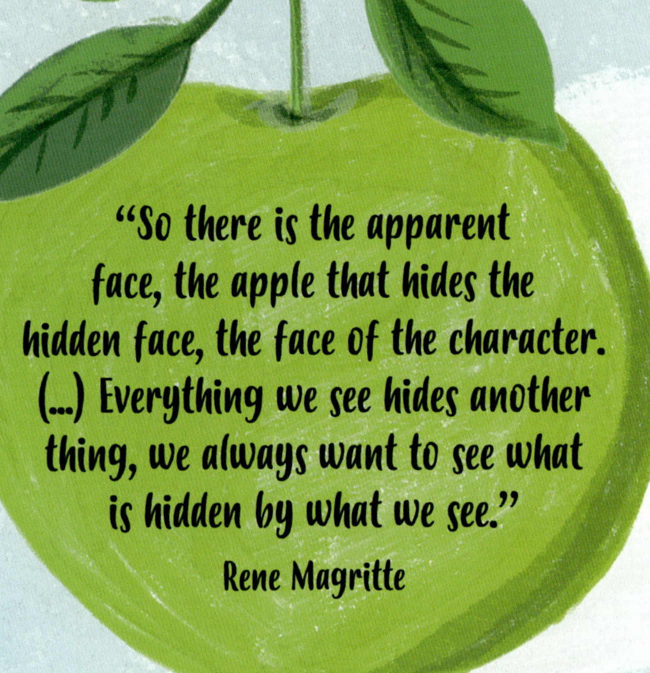

EDEN'S APPLE

A recurring emblem in Magritte's work, the apple is a reference to the garden of Eden and brings to mind original sin – the figure in the image is literally blinded by sin.

EYE OF REMEMBRANCE

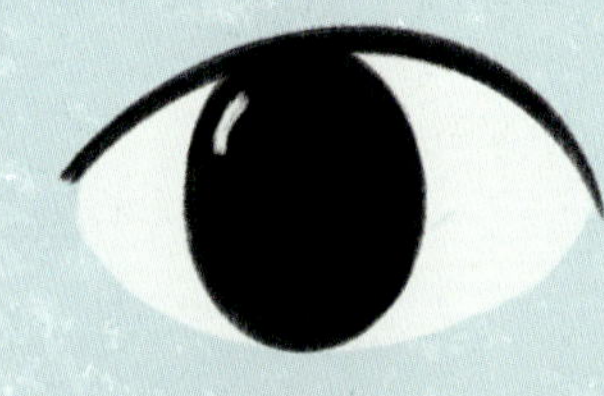

Thought to be a symbol of mourning for the painter, the partially visible eye recalls his mother's appearance – she died when Magritte was a teenager.

BRICK WALL

The wall acts as a barrier between the earthly and the celestial and is also suggestive of concealment.

GREY SKIES

In contrast to the calm, serene sea, the
sky looks like a storm is rolling in, about
to engulf the man.

BOWLER HAT

Many critics have seen this work as a late
self-portrait of the artist, as he was often seen
dressed in a bowler hat and red tie. As an
artist he was dismissive of this narcissistic
theme, which could explain why he hides the
face of the subject behind the apple.

RED TIE

The rich, deep red of the man's tie speaks
of power; the combination of the tie and
apple could be perceived as a comment
on the corrupting quality of power.

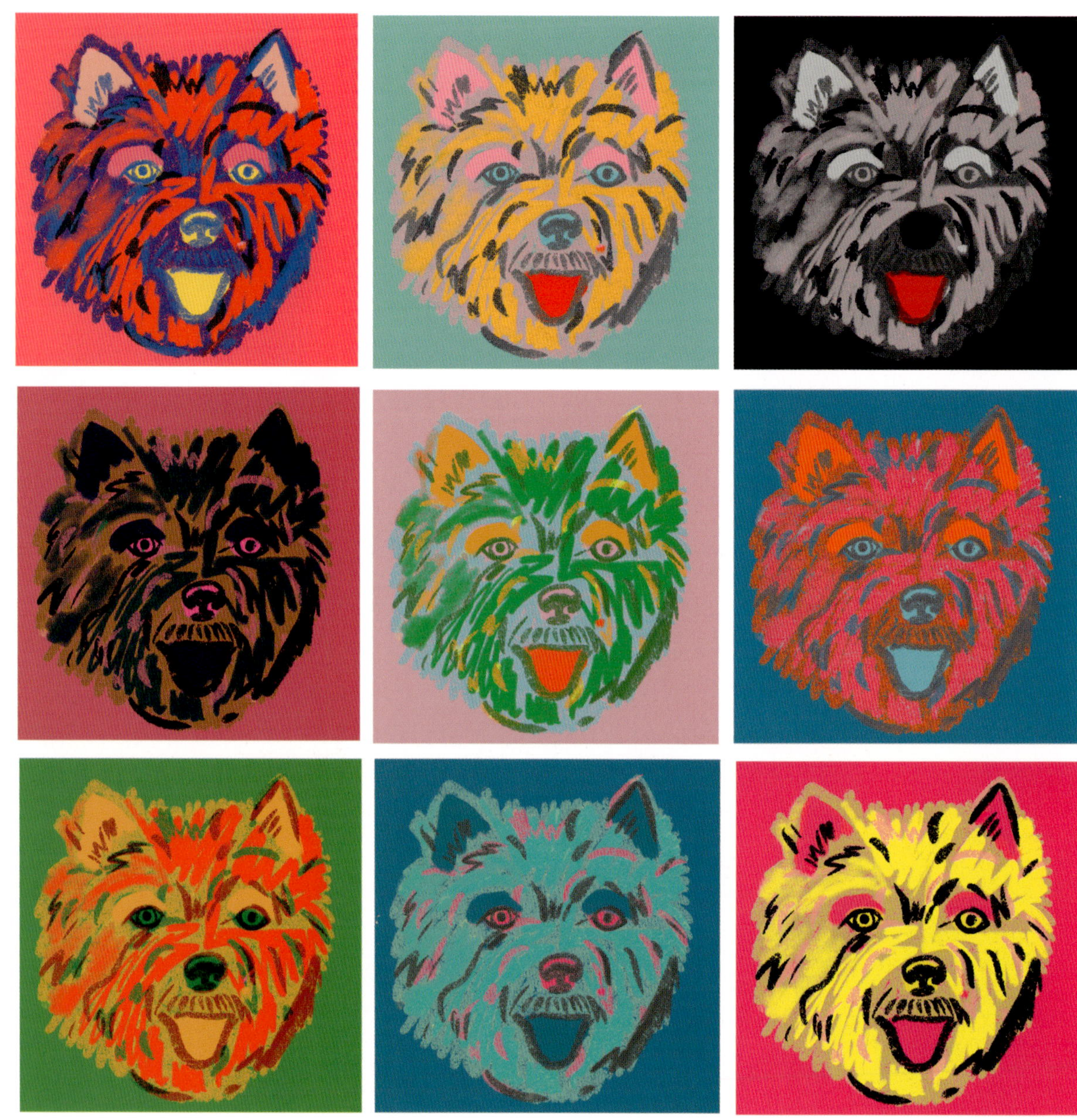

MARILYN
BY ANDY WARHOL

The 1967 Marilyn Monroe screenprints by Andy Warhol are some of the most well-known artworks in the world. Based on his original silk screen *Marilyn Diptych* of 1962, their bright, eye-catching palette, combined with the subject – one of the most famous film stars of the era – proved to be an unstoppable combination. Individual prints have changed hands for hundreds of thousands of pounds up until the present day.

Demonstrating Warhol's preoccupation with glamour, fame and mass media, the portraits have become an icon of the 1960s and the Pop Art movement in general. The Pop Artist's obsession with celebrity, beauty and death are all cleverly channelled into these portraits of Monroe.

Part of Warhol's success lay in his understanding of art as a commercial medium. Screenprinting paintings that he had previously painstakingly created by hand, his 'Factory Editions' portfolios, featuring garish combinations of Day-Glo paints, have become synonymous with the graphic style of the Pop Art movement.

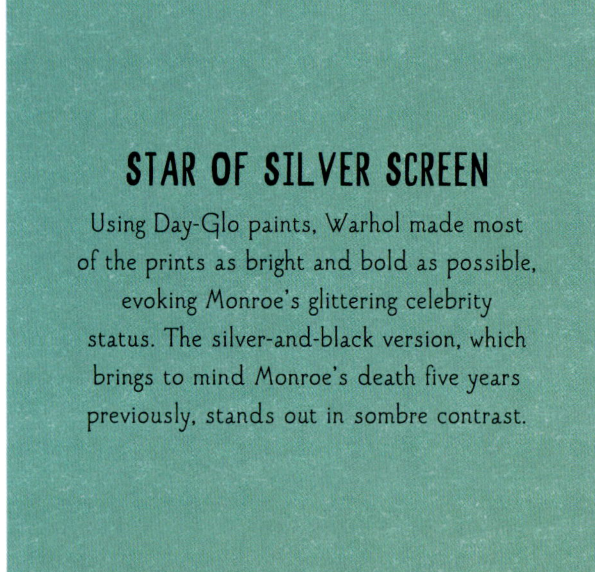

STAR OF SILVER SCREEN

Using Day-Glo paints, Warhol made most
of the prints as bright and bold as possible,
evoking Monroe's glittering celebrity
status. The silver-and-black version, which
brings to mind Monroe's death five years
previously, stands out in sombre contrast.

STRIKING LIPS

Vibrantly coloured to reflect her vivacious
personality, Warhol draws attention to
Monroe's trademark pout, highlighting
her well-known status.

"The idea is not to live forever;
it is to create something that will."

Andy Warhol

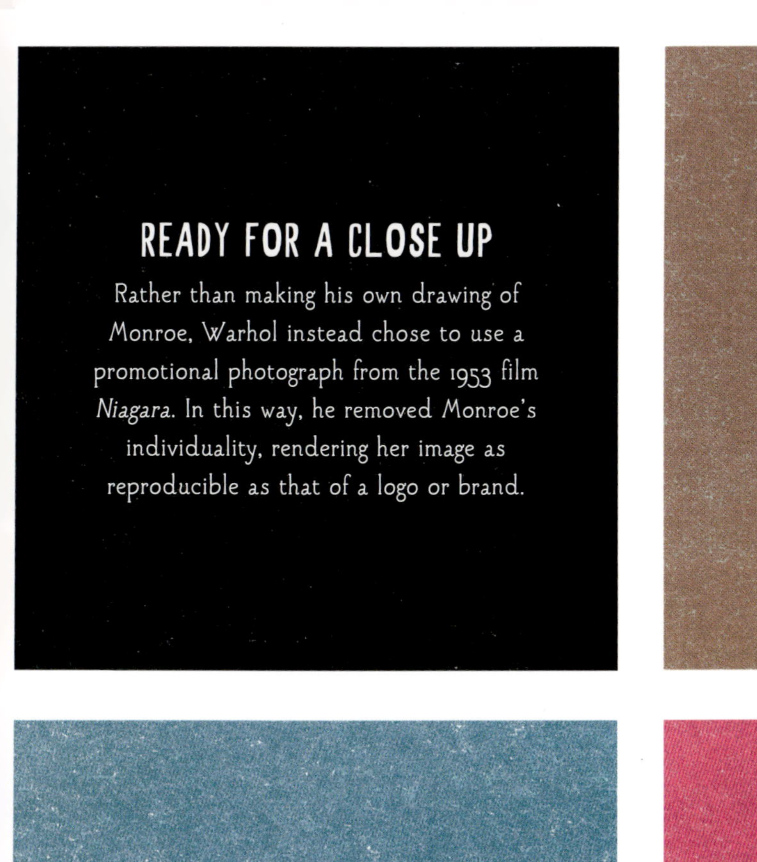

READY FOR A CLOSE UP

Rather than making his own drawing of
Monroe, Warhol instead chose to use a
promotional photograph from the 1953 film
Niagara. In this way, he removed Monroe's
individuality, rendering her image as
reproducible as that of a logo or brand.

REPEATED IMAGES

Warhol was interested in how mass
production decreases perceived
value. Through his portraits he deftly
demonsrates how Monroe's ubiquity meant
that she was somehow seen as less than
human, defined merely by her fame and
public persona.

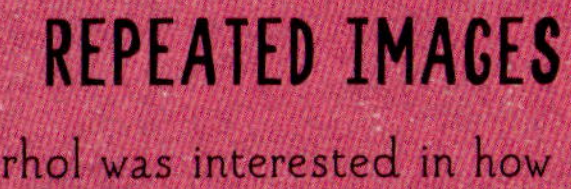

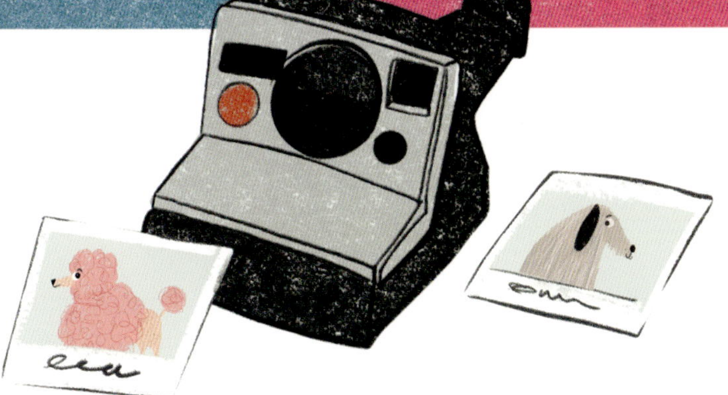

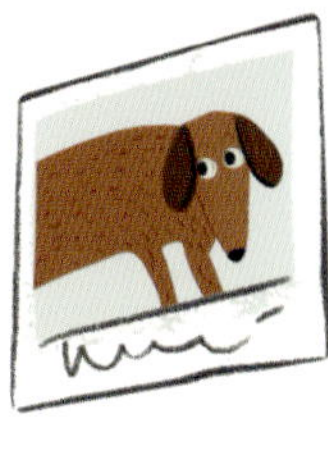

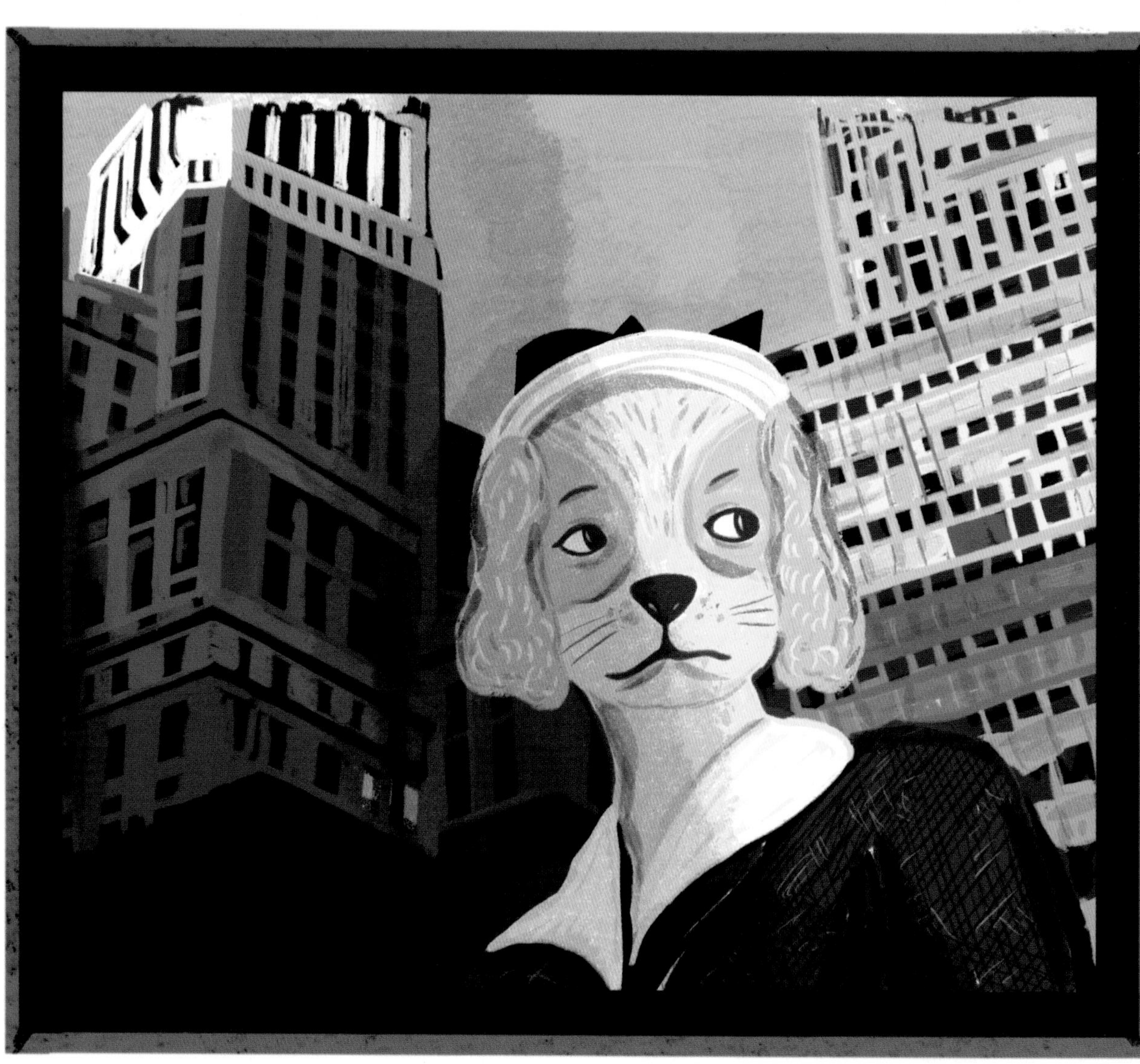

UNTITLED FILM STILL #21 BY CINDY SHERMAN

Photographer Cindy Sherman is known for her challenging depictions of gender, which often highlight stereotypes and prejudices. She is widely recognized as one of the most important and influential artists of the late twentieth and early twenty-first centuries.

Between 1977 and 1980, Sherman photographed herself in a series of scenarios based on contemporary Hollywood tropes. *Untitled Film Still #21* brings to mind the films of Alfred Hitchcock, featuring a 'career girl' alone on the streets of the big city. In doing so, Sherman produced a subtle satire of feminine stereotypes and compelled viewers to recognize the damaging effects of reducing women to mere caricatures.

Sherman's reimagining of the medium of portraiture, which had fallen out of fashion by the twentieth century, has influenced not only photographers but also painters, sculptors and performance artists, making this groundbreaking series one of the most important bodies of work in contemporary art.

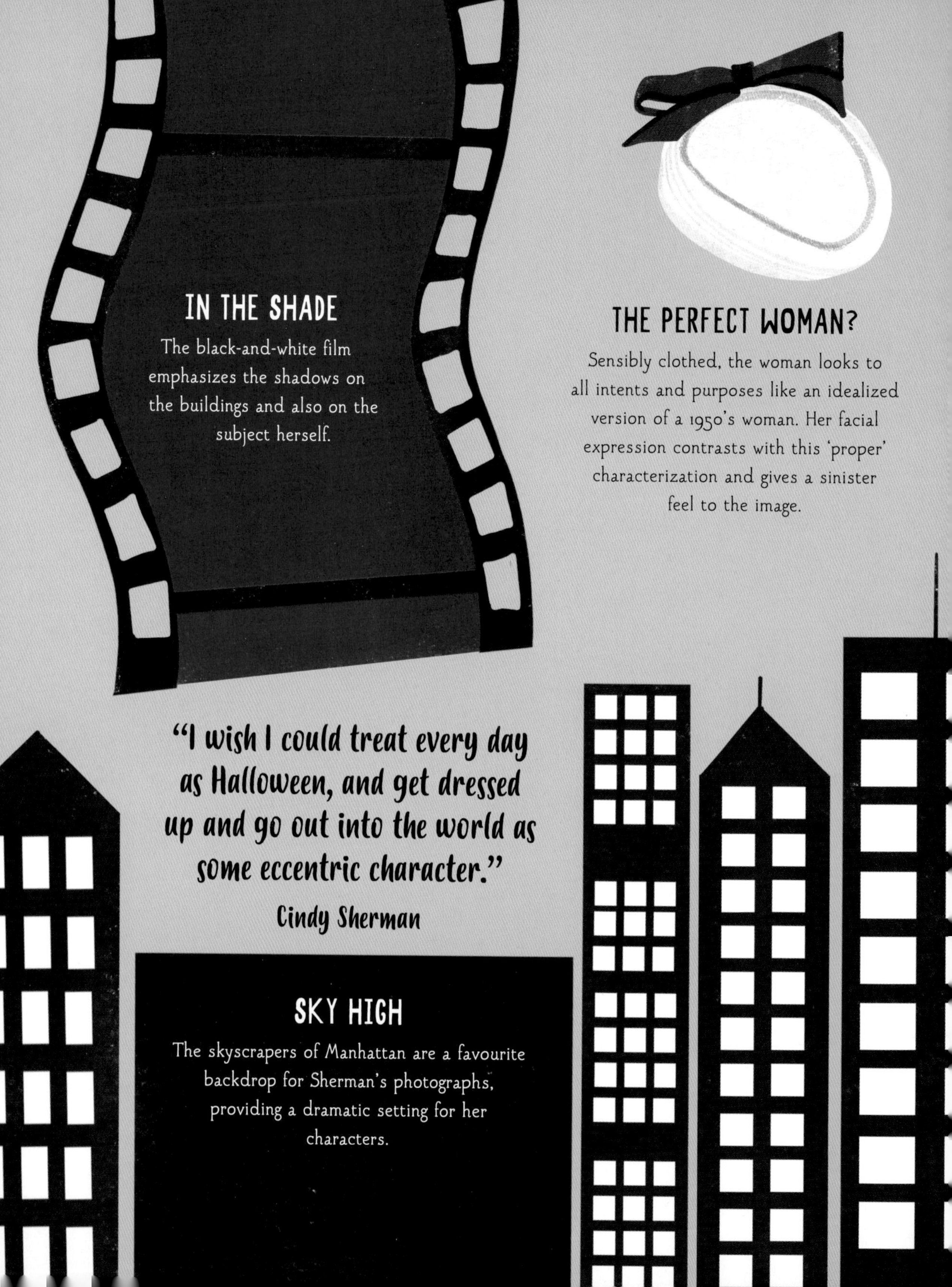

IN THE SHADE

The black-and-white film emphasizes the shadows on the buildings and also on the subject herself.

THE PERFECT WOMAN?

Sensibly clothed, the woman looks to all intents and purposes like an idealized version of a 1950's woman. Her facial expression contrasts with this 'proper' characterization and gives a sinister feel to the image.

"I wish I could treat every day as Halloween, and get dressed up and go out into the world as some eccentric character."

Cindy Sherman

SKY HIGH

The skyscrapers of Manhattan are a favourite backdrop for Sherman's photographs, providing a dramatic setting for her characters.

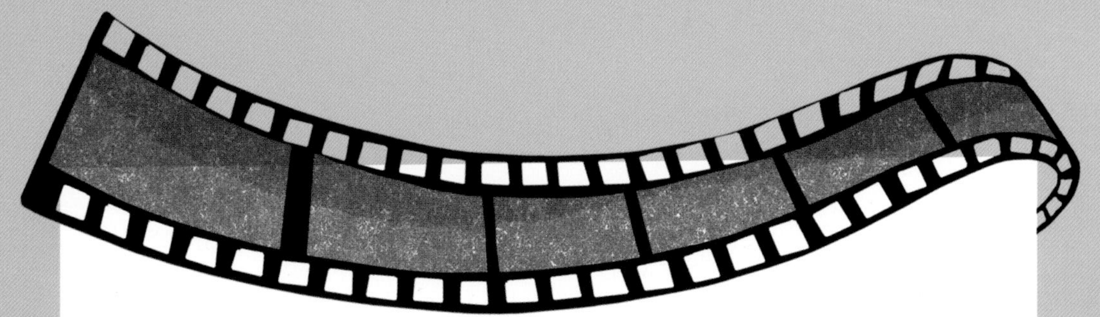

SELFIE STYLE

The 'selfie' has come a long way since chemist Robert Cornelius took the first-known photographic self-portrait in 1839. Technology may have moved on since then, but the urge to capture self-likenesses on film has only grown stronger.

While many selfies are taken merely to capture a moment of fun, Cindy Sherman's shapeshifting self-portraits sought to draw attention to the oppressive influence of mass media over our individual and collective identities. By transforming her appearance through make-up, costumes, and prosthetics, she created powerful and often unsettling images. Her photographs explore themes of identity and prejudice, questioning societal norms and the viewer's subconscious preconceptions.

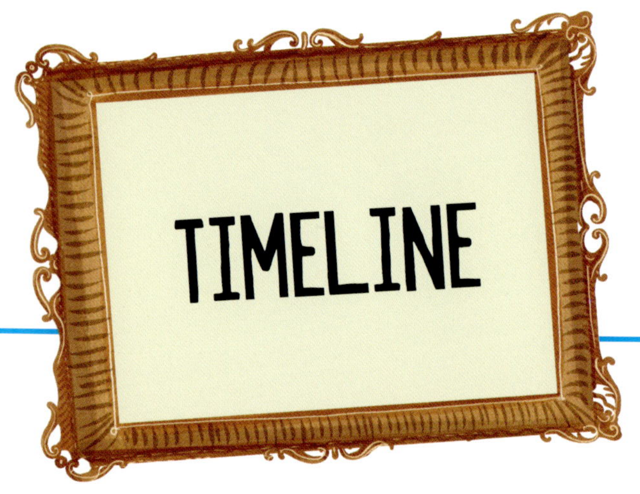

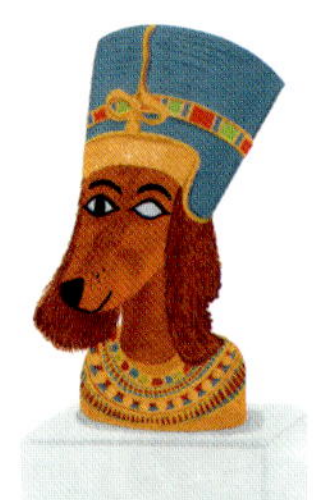

1340 BCE
The Bust of Nefertiti
Ancient Egyptian Art

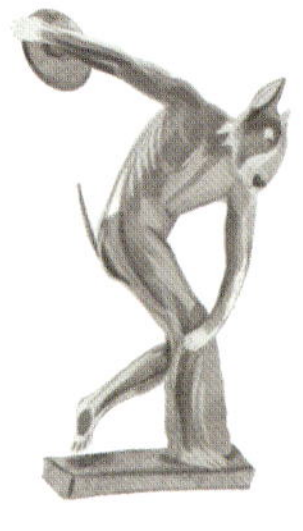

450 BCE
Discobolus
Ancient Greek Art

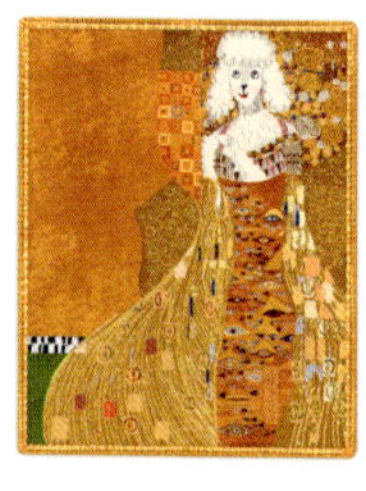

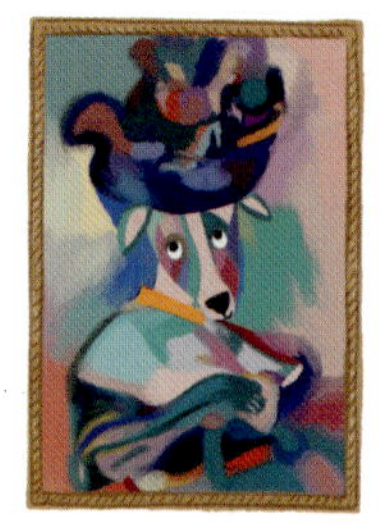

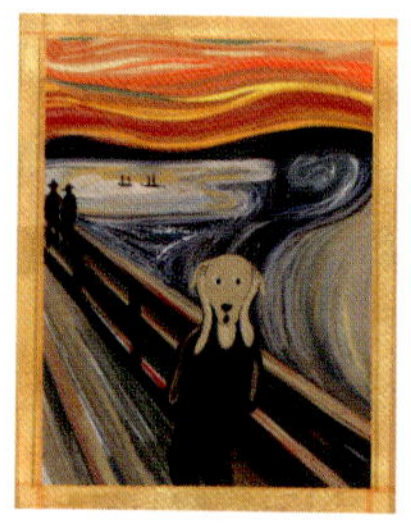

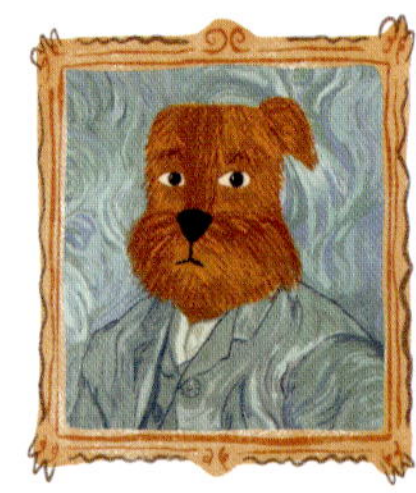

1907
*Portrait of Adele
Bloch-Bauer I*
Symbolism

1905
Woman with a Hat
Fauvism

1893
The Scream
Expressionism

1889
Self-Portrait 1889
Post-Impressionism

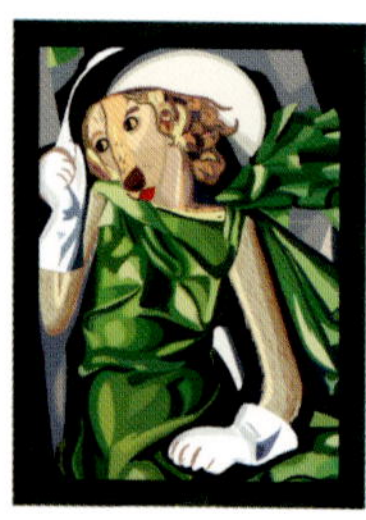

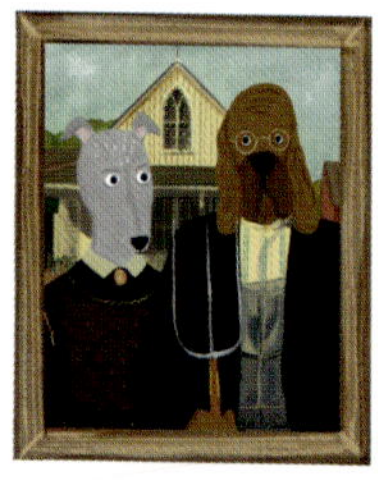

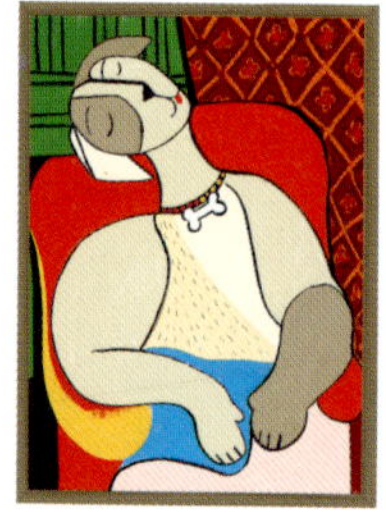

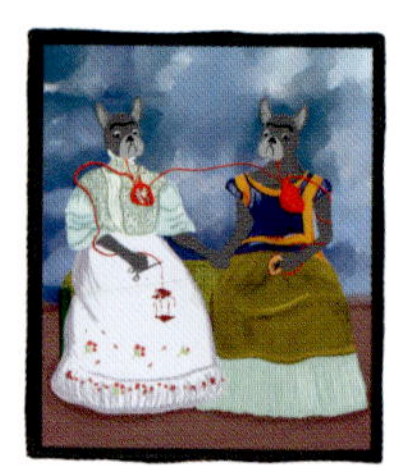

1930
*Young Lady
with Gloves*
Art Deco

1930
American Gothic
Social Realism

1932
The Dream
Cubism

1939
The Two Fridas
Magic Realism

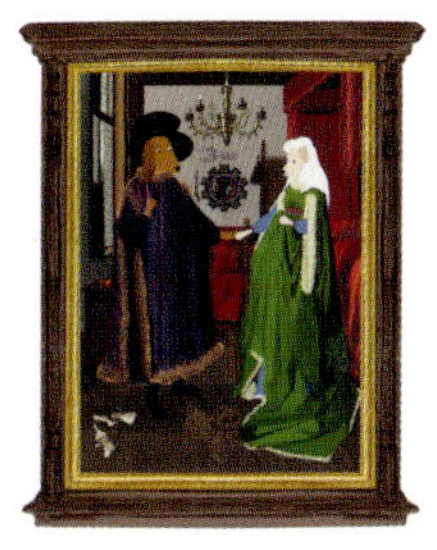

1434
The Arnolfini Portrait
Northern Renaissance

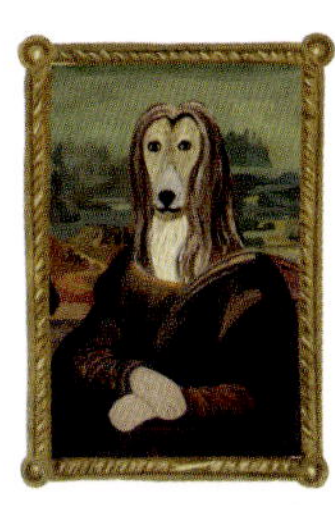

1503–1519
Mona Lisa
High Renaissance

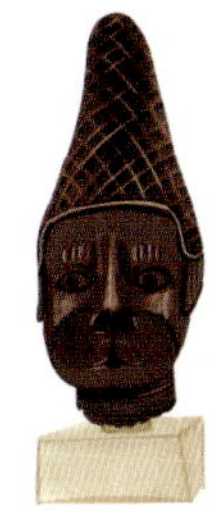

16TH CENTURY
*Bronze Head
of Queen Idia*
Benin Kingdom

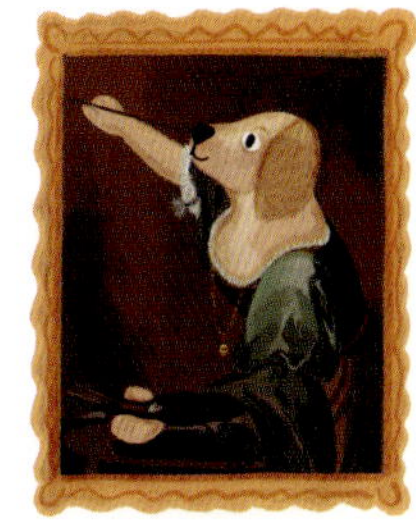

1639
Self-Portrait
Baroque

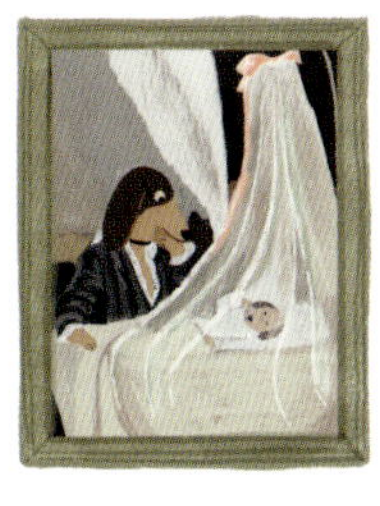

1872
The Cradle
Impressionism

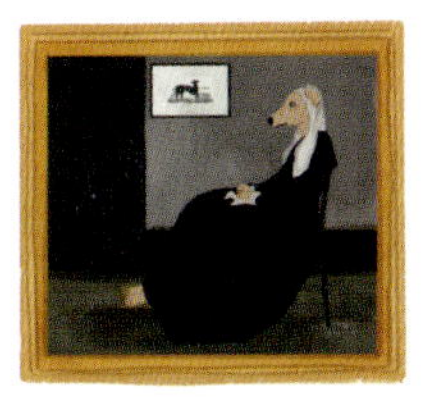

1871
*Arrangement in Grey
and Black No. 1*
American Gilded Age

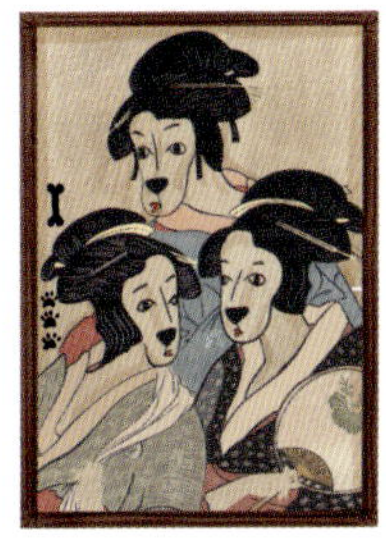

1791
*Three Beauties of the
Present Day*
Edo

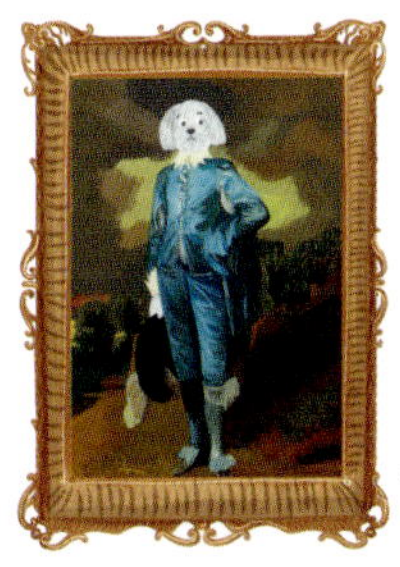

1770
The Blue Boy
Rococo

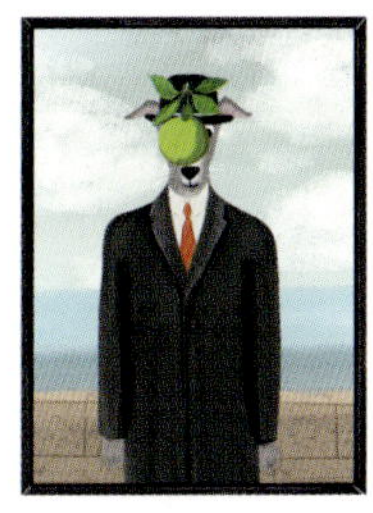

1964
The Son of Man
Surrealism

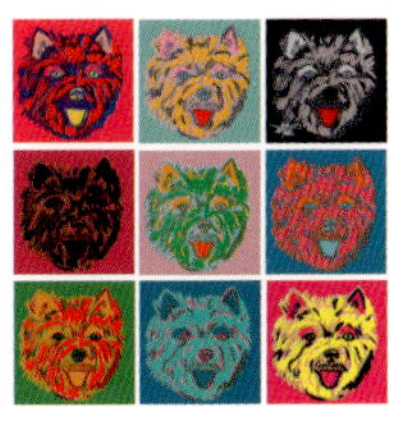

1967
Marilyn
Pop Art

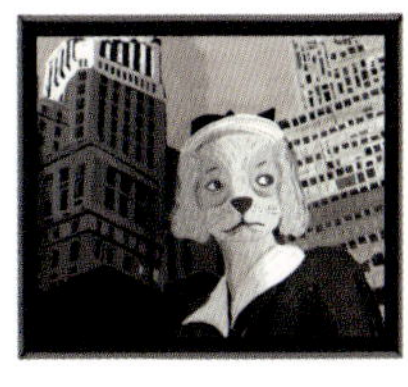

1977
Untitled Film Still #21
Photography

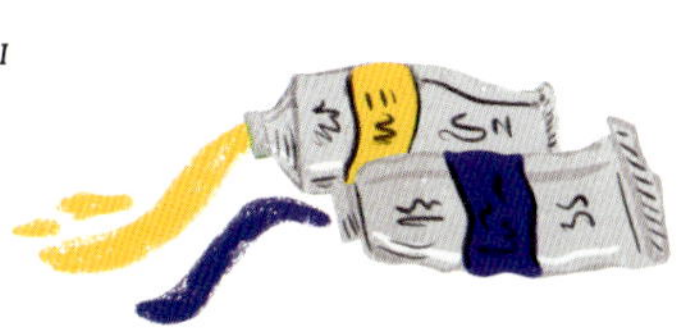